MW00612059

# SMALL SPACE REVOLUTION

In honor of my late mother who embodies past and present, in spirit, and to my children who inspire present and future.

**DK**

# SMALL SPACE REVOLUTION

## PLANTING SEEDS OF CHANGE IN YOUR COMMUNITY

Tayshan Hayden-Smith

# CONTENTS

# A CALL TO ACTION

I hope this book serves you as a safe space for experimentation; to try something new; to see life through a different lens; to think about a different approach—maybe a slight shift in mindset; to just simply "be"; and to offer a perspective of hope.

It's true that I don't know it all, and I definitely don't have all of the answers. I am here to learn; to be inspired; to be in awe; to appreciate and understand as much as I possibly can; and to try to be positive; to look at solutions; and to find joy through nature. In the same way that I'm stepping out of my comfort zone in order to write this book, I urge you, at the very least, to take inspiration from the many ideas, projects, and case study examples from inspiring people and special spaces.

This book channels the positive energy of my late mother, Nancy, who was, and still is, a constant reminder of how kind, nurturing, and caring the world can be. When growing up, I saw with my own eyes just how infectious her beauty was. Being a true leader through love, mum taught her children respect and humility; we were always told to live without limitations, (nearly) without rules, as well as to be fearless, bold, and confident. I believe that those lessons have encouraged me to *just do*—I'm still working on the *just be* bit, though. My life has been full of twists, turns, trials, and tribulations, and I'm sure there are many still to come.

*Small Space Revolution* is all about finding the balance between the dreamy, hazy, and emotive approach to life, and the actionable, science-driven, and tangible one. Yes, nature can be all lovely and flowery, but, even more so, it's crucial that we see it as an opportunity to support people and planet, whether it's by designing safe structures and buildings or by etching out spaces for pollinators—the future is in our hands. There's something amazing about the human race that allows us to manipulate, guide, and accelerate what would otherwise be much slower natural processes. Let's use that to our advantage.

Now it's my turn, as a young father to two children, to hand down that baton to teach, share, and grow, but equally to listen, understand, and accommodate. Being a young person today is a constant uphill battle—trust me. Every seed that's planted as a result of this book will bloom and flourish. And if it doesn't, that's also okay—may it be the fertile ground to spark more conversation, ideas, and action. I hope to lead by example, but I know I won't always get it right. So take this as a gentle nudge—not only to me but also to all of you—to say let's just *try*.

# RECONNECT

/ˌriː.kəˈnekt/

**Reconnect**
verb
to link together again

# NATURE

# HAD COME
# TO MY

# RESCUE

Wandering through my community—North Kensington (West London)—I am constantly, subconsciously, and rudely interrupted by my everyday scenery. Let's call it out for what it is—it is, undeniably, an unwanted attraction. Yet, I am torn because it's what I've always known—it's familiar. The places we have come to call home are overwhelmed by the red bricks of buildings that tower high; the tarmac that consumes the road; the glass storefronts glaring at you. As an inner-city boy, born and raised, I have only just come to realize how brutal and cold my everyday experience is. Nature has become underappreciated and is consequently under attack by us. I don't think we quite realize the extent of the effect our environment has on both our mental and physical health. Can you imagine the subconscious and psychological impact of a disconnect with the natural world? Do you ever think about what effect that has on you? Is this what the future looks like?

Furthermore, what could you do about it? How did we get here?

The journey for me thus far has not been the smoothest—to say the least. I say that, not as a complaint but in reflection. There have often been moments of trauma and tragedy that have really made me ask the most difficult questions of myself—questions of purpose, legacy, and justice. 2017 proved to be one of the biggest tests of my resilience and will. The Grenfell Tower fire took lives and changed lives in my community. As a result, I asked myself: who was I? What did I stand for? What was I doing this for? What legacy did I want to leave?

Nature was the catalyst for me beginning to understand myself enough to start answering some of those questions, after what had been one of the most challenging moments of my life. With no plan or strategy, I took to the streets, among others in the community. It wasn't long before I stumbled into a derelict, unused, barren piece of land that would soon become my place of healing in the months following. Nature had come to my rescue. As the garden began to grow, so did we. I then went on to reclaim five spaces in the community through guerrilla gardening—meeting people from all backgrounds, religions, ages, and cultures in those spaces.

I keenly felt the injustices of the Grenfell Tower fire and was forced to confront the reality that 72 human beings who were my neighbors, friends, and members of the community—people I knew, connected with, and passed every day: women, men, and children—were no longer here to fulfill the dreams that they had, the lives they had to live, and the love they had to share. It was with this in mind that I was driven to fight for a better society—one that would work for people and planet.

I guess it all started before 2017, though. I've always counted myself as lucky to have had my late mum as a bold, brave influence and inspiration. My mother, Nancy, was a single mother to four of us—it's fair to say that there was never a dull moment in the Hayden-Smith household. I'm really not sure how she managed and coped with us four. Dubbed supermum by many other parents at school, she really was a light that shone, not only at home but also at school and in the community. Walking down the road with my mum would never be quick. Hours of conversation, laughter, and tears would commence as she stopped to chat with, what felt like, every single person living in the community of North Kensington. Little did I know at the time, but these were the moments that emphasized the very values of community, and getting to know and understand the people in it, that became instilled in us, although you'd often find us four impatient children arguing and fighting in the midst of these "catch ups" my mum would be having.

It wasn't just people that my mum had an innate ability to connect and sympathize with; it was very much nature that increasingly became central to our way of life. Due to a terminal cancer diagnosis in 2010, we saw our mum fight her

# I'VE COME TO REALIZE THAT WE MUST RECONNECT AT ALL COSTS WITH EACH OTHER AND WITH NATURE—BOTH EQUALLY

way through life so gracefully with a really positive outlook on everything. My mum became known for stopping everyone in her tracks to spotlight and magnify the beauty of our natural surroundings—even if at the time I did act disinterested and grumpy. I wish she knew just how much her fascination and insight had impacted on my curious mind. It's those very rare glimpses into the magic of nature that sparked a very young Tayshan's interest and love for nature, which continues to take my breath away, even on the busiest, most chaotic of days. Whether it's a building engulfed by the wandering wisteria; or the camouflage-like trunks of the London plane trees; or the dramatic, painted sunset sky; it is within the safety of nature that my mother's spirit is embedded, cherished, and it will always be a route for me to connect with her.

Now at 27 years of age, I've come to realize that we must reconnect at all costs with each other and with nature—both equally as important as each other, going hand in hand. There's no other way or alternative. Through connection comes understanding, compassion, and community. I always think that societal pressures, technological advances, and the fast-pace, consumerist ways of the world are driving us to a disconnect never seen before, leaving our communities soulless and the environment in a crisis. If there ever has been an opportunity to try and find that connection, now is the time to look beyond the barriers, boundaries, and walls put before you.

# HANDS
# OFF

# MANGROVE

BY GROW TO KNOW
RHS CHELSEA FLOWER SHOW, LONDON, UK

Grow to Know, born in response to the Grenfell Tower fire in North Kensington, London, set out to reclaim spaces and reconnect people with nature and each other. Just ten minutes down the road (and in the same London borough), one of the most prestigious horticultural events in the world takes place every year. In 2022, Grow to Know designed their own garden at the RHS Chelsea Flower Show. It was intended to be a statement garden—one to evoke conversation, debate, and renewed thinking—and that's exactly what it did.

The Hands Off Mangrove garden raised awareness of the intersectional issues of the social injustice surrounding the Mangrove Nine and the environmental problems of deforestation in mangrove forests. The former was a very local story, in Notting Hill, while the other was a global one about our detrimental impacts on the natural environment. We all have a massive part to play in both issues, here, today.

A garden pivoting on coexistence and connection, such as the Hands Off Mangrove, was one for all—a community garden to welcome people no matter their background, as well as wildlife, big and small. RHS Chelsea Flower Show was merely a showcase for this garden, which would come to find a permanent home in North Kensington.

Its brutal, stark, deforested mangrove sculpture towered 14½ ft (4.5 m) tall and had nine roots reaching into the soil—each representing a Mangrove Nine defendant. The absence of a mangrove trunk was not to be ignored. Typically, a trunk is a sanctuary for many wild animals and the lungs of the earth, as well as a safe, vibrant, community space such as The Mangrove restaurant in Notting Hill. The mere existence of such spaces to coexist is key to our future.

Grow to Know gave the stage to nature through its biodiverse range of plants, ensuring nature was the client we were responding to as the design unfolded. Imperfections that would otherwise be marked down at Chelsea Flower Show were celebrated in our garden—with "pests" and insects welcome.

"What plant is that?" "What's the name of that tree?" "What's this garden about?" As visitors crowded into the garden, many were in awe at all the beautiful plants. Gardening was our common ground. It's what brought us all together—a shared interest and passion. It was nature that became the soft entry point to discussion around typically sensitive topics such as climate change, police brutality, and racism.

While the messaging behind this RHS Chelsea Flower Show garden could be seen as quite heavy and disheartening, it was important that people came away from it with a positive feeling—one of optimism to come together to share, learn, and coexist, both with nature and each other.

## WHO WERE THE MANGROVE NINE?

The Mangrove restaurant in Notting Hill, named in tribute to the beautiful mangroves in Trinidad, became a fertile ground for activism, resistance, and resilience as Frank Crichlow, owner of The Mangrove, took a stand together with Barbara Beese, Altheia Jones-LeCointe, Darcus Howe, Rupert Boyce, Elton Anthony Inniss, Rothwell Kentish, Godfrey Millett, and Rhodan Gordon against the Metropolitan Police. Dubbed the Mangrove Nine, they set out to seek justice and take action on the relentless police brutality and racism endured at The Mangrove, since it had opened in 1968, and nationwide. In Darcus Howe's own words: "We've complained to the

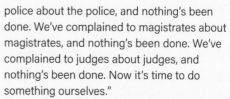

police about the police, and nothing's been done. We've complained to magistrates about magistrates, and nothing's been done. We've complained to judges about judges, and nothing's been done. Now it's time to do something ourselves."

In 1970, some 150 people took to the streets in support of the Mangrove Nine. At that time, Black people were targeted simply for the color of their skin, so this was a brave stand to make—it was called The Frontline on All Saints Road. Inevitably, the Mangrove Nine were subsequently arrested and were charged with a whole array of crimes. After enduring a 55-day trial, with most of the Nine representing themselves legally, the Mangrove Nine were acquitted of their most egregious charges and, crucially, it was the first ever acknowledgment of behavior motivated by racial hatred within the Metropolitan Police—evoking much-needed change from within the force. However, it is important not to view with rose-tinted glasses this milestone victory in the fight for equality, as the experiences of the Mangrove Nine had negative and lasting impacts on them, their families, and the local community.

## WHAT CAN YOU DO?

Feel empowered to share your thoughts, ideas, and stories with like-minded and not so like-minded people. Our differences should be celebrated, and the Hands Off Mangrove garden existed to do that.

## In conversation with Danny Clarke

Since our first collaboration, creating a guerrilla garden for RHS Chelsea Flower Show 2022, Danny Clarke has become codirector at Grow to Know.

**TAYSHAN: Last year, we were at RHS Chelsea Flower Show, where we created the Hands Off Mangrove garden. And I just wanted to get a feel of what it meant for you.**

**DANNY:** Really, the Hands Off Mangrove garden, to me, was about paying homage to the West Indians that came to this country in the early '50s, as well as paying tribute to their resilience and bravery. And it was a real privilege to be able to tell the story through a garden, and to do this at the heart of horticulture, through the RHS at the Chelsea Flower Show.

**TAYSHAN: And do you think storytelling has a massive part to play in how we interact with gardens, nature, and outdoor spaces in general?**

**DANNY:** Absolutely. I think this sort of storytelling is very important. Because we need to know our history, we should understand where we're coming from, in order to move forward. What is the past? The present is only a split second, isn't it? And then it's gone. So, really, our life consists of the past and what's to come in the future. The present is almost nonexistent.

**TAYSHAN: But nature helps you enjoy that present moment.**

**DANNY:** Yes, it brings you into a moment, doesn't it? I mean, that's the thing with nature. When I'm gardening, I'm not thinking about everything else that's going on. I'm just concentrating on what I'm planting, sowing the seeds, putting the bulbs in the ground, trimming a hedge or whatever, or also listening to the birds tweet. It's a very very momentary experience—and it's there to enjoy for us all.

# STREET PLANTING

## THINK ABOUT WHAT YOUR ROAD COULD LOOK LIKE. HOW DOES IT MAKE YOU FEEL?

Any space has the potential to be a garden or, at the very least, an opportunity for nature to creep in—you'll be surprised what can grow where. It was only recently I stumbled across a fully formed and fruiting tomato plant growing between the cracks of a sidewalk in inner-city London, also neighbored by a vibrant chard plant. Something tells me that there's a gardener behind this curious experiment, and while it's impractical to start planting between every crevice on roads and streets (although I'm not against it!), such seemingly random planting really does exemplify the resilience of plants. They, as well as humans, have had to adapt to the ever-increasing temperatures in towns and cities because of climate change—worsened by the development of urban infrastructure, which absorbs and reemits the sun's heat. Growing plants on streets can be an invaluable way forward in helping to reduce temperatures, benefiting both planet and people.

Think about what your road could look like. How does it make you feel? I always view spaces with a green to gray ratio in mind—where does your road sit on that? What percentage of it is green?

The two main opportunities to plant in your street are: to use an existing space; and to create a planting space from scratch.

⮕ Under this tree I planted gerbera, ferns, heuchera, and some bulbs, as well as mahonia, hellebore, and periwinkle nearby.

## PLANTING IDEAS FOR THE BASE OF AN ESTABLISHED TREE

—

- O  Ferns
- O  Japanese spurge (*Pachysandra terminalis*)
- O  Lady's mantle (*Alchemilla mollis*)
- O  Lesser periwinkle (*Vinca minor*)
- O  Mahonia (*Mahonia*)
- O  Plantain lily (*Hosta*)
- O  Sweet box (*Sarcococca*)
- O  Siberian bugloss (*Brunnera macrophylla*)
- O  Snowdrop (*Galanthus*)
- O  Wood anemone (*Anemone nemorosa*)

## PLANTING UNDER A TREE

Think carefully and realistically about the size of the space you have identified, what plant or plants might be appropriate, and if there is anything already growing there. Choose a plant that won't compete with or outgrow the tree. Often the base of the tree can be shady, so select plants that can cope with such conditions.

To give any plants the best start, aim to plant in fall or spring, when temperatures aren't extreme and there is soft, moisture-filled soil for roots to establish in. Never plant in very dry or frozen soil. Use a trowel or bulb planter to dig the planting holes, being careful not to damage any tree roots. When planting under a tree, choose small plug plants or bulbs, which can establish in the pockets between the roots. Do not plant bulbs under evergreen trees which will reduce the amount of light reaching the ground and will impact the beautiful bloom moment we all look forward to.

Ensure your new plants are well watered until they are established. Conveniently, there are telltale signs that indicate just how healthy and established your plant is. A thriving plant will exhibit vibrant, green leaves; new shoots coming through; and a strong root system, which navigates deeply—as opposed to being exposed on the surface.

## CREATING A PLANTING SPACE

When creating a new space to plant in a built-up area, you can get really creative by, for example, using upcycled pots, trash cans, rubber tires, or pretty much anything. However, the planter must be big enough for your plant to grow into a healthy specimen, whether it be a tree, bushy shrub, edibles, or small perennial pollinator.

Be sure to identify a spot where your installation doesn't obstruct access. It could be out beside your front door or on your street. Test your idea by considering aspect first (whether it's sunny or shady) and what it is you're growing, and, if it's not a good location, look for a different spot.

When being grown in a container, a plant will need more regular watering, particularly during dry spells, compared to plants in the open ground. Therefore, consider choosing low-maintenance and resilient plants for containers, depending on how much time you have for plant care.

## PLANTING IDEAS FOR CONTAINERS
—

**Shade lovers:**
- Aeonium (*Aeonium*)
- Common ragwort (*Senecio jacobaea*)
- Ferns

**Sun seekers:**
- Coneflower (*Echinacea*)
- Fescue (*Festuca*)
- Hebe (*Hebe*)
- Osteospermum (*Osteospermum*)
- Phormium (*Phormium*)
- Sea holly (*Eryngium*)
- Stonecrop (*Hylotelephium*, syn. *Sedum*)
- Yarrow (*Achillea*)

◉ Here I have grown edibles such as beets (*in the front*), fennel (*right*), and chard (*at the back*).

/ˌriːˈθɪŋk/

# RETHINK

**Rethink**
*verb*
to think about a plan, idea,
or system again, especially
in order to change or
improve it

# WHAT LESSONS ARE WE PASSING ON TO OUR CHILDREN?

6.20

6.10

6

5.50

What does a classroom represent to you? What did your own classroom look like? Chairs—blue and plastic, by any chance? You know the ones ... Desks or tables—perhaps also with a plastic, vinyl, faux-wood table top and gray metal poles as legs? Maybe a whiteboard? Into such a fixed space, a child will go every day, yet this intended hub of learning to inspire, captivate, and excite the child is all so formal, rigid, and sanitized. What lessons are we passing on to the younger generations as we confine them within the four walls of a classroom and impose endless rules and routine: do this, do that, don't do this, don't do that? We're blindly putting our children through a relentless, overwhelming, outdated system where we deprive those very children not only of relevant and up-to-date knowledge and information but also, most importantly, of space and freedom.

Everything has been made to impose, rush, and panic—I don't think we quite comprehend the amount of pressure children are under. But what if the idea of a classroom was more fluid, flexible, and free? If a playground was a classroom? What about a garden? Or a park? The local community? If we're going to even start thinking about a shift in culture and behavior toward each other, as a people and the environment, surely the first place to start is in schools and in education.

If the COVID-19 pandemic in 2020 taught us anything, it was how important outdoor green spaces are for the many benefits that being in nature emphasize—especially to those who may have limited access. Owning a garden, of any size, is a luxury that, unfortunately, many cannot afford. With schools being the prime places of learning and of curiosity and a central access point for children across the nations, how could you argue with the lessons that even just simply being in nature bring, and why are we not introducing nature into the classroom more often—or using it as the classroom?

The release of joy, the feeling of freedom, the chance for your imagination to run wild and to breathe in fresh air, and the opportunity to explore and embark on mini adventures are just a few glimpses into the dramatically contrasting magical landscape of the outdoors compared with the everyday indoor classroom. Thus, children would be able to escape the restrictions and pressures of the curriculum. Surely, the curriculum, along with exam culture, is in need of a serious rethink. For me, it is a no-brainer to ensure, at the very least, weekly allowances for outdoor play, outdoor learning, and, dare I say it, mischief.

But nature isn't just a good release or escape. There are some really important lessons to be learned through nature. The processes of life, the seasons, and the transitions are all very symbolic and prominent throughout every single person's life—it is important to emphasize that we are not detached from nature. We are nature. We are the changing seasons, and as we came to the earth as a speck of dust we will one day return to the earth as a speck of dust.

Understanding these processes is crucial in helping us judge ourselves and to see why it's our responsibility to nurture our relationship with nature. Such an assessment can also reflect and shine a light on what should be, the very sacred values of how we take care of each other and our personal relationships.

Our relationship with the land is all but lost, especially in the city, but how can you blame a child for that? Where are the opportunities? Who are the influences? What is being put before children? What are we prioritizing? You'd be very surprised just how many children think that their food comes from a sealed plastic bag on a shelf in a store—this breaks my heart.

With cities becoming food deserts and fresh, organic food made to feel like a luxury often sold beyond the price limit of the majority, there is so much power in knowing how to grow your own food—no matter how much space you have. "Growing your own food is like printing your own money," according to community gardener Ron

Finley (see p.158). Growing food feels like it should be a fundamental skill, yet it has been made unreachable, a luxury, and a hobby at best. The irrefutable power in being able to not only grow your own food but also possess the culinary skills to turn that food into a nourishing, wholesome meal is priceless—especially in this day and age, where these are unfortunately dying arts, particularly in and among younger generations. This begs the question: why are these not compulsory in schools?

My point is that every day we miss many chances to enhance and harness that very raw and uncensored admiration for nature in children (and adults!)—it all seems a bit too obvious to ignore, doesn't it? If we're going to adapt and maneuver with the impact of climate change, we need more advocates of nature, the environment, and community—more changemakers and leaders.

Every person has the potential to change the world, and our duty is to give them the tools, the resources, and the ideas to inspire them so they can influence and reclaim their futures, currently stolen through greed, profit, and power. Nature is a riddle begging to be explored, understood, and sought—but, most of all, respected. Not every question is answerable, and that's okay—it's fine to let the mind wander, journey, and navigate through the intricacies and also the vagueness of the universe. Everyday is a new day to learn. Who said that education ends at school? More than anything, our interaction with nature brings out the child in us. The colors, the textures, the elements. We are all students of life but we must be in control of the experiences that we are opening ourselves up to learn from. Our everyday experience is not meant to be so rigid and sanitized. Work with nature, interact with it—no day will ever be the same. In my experience, that is often when the mind is most fertile for planting those seeds of change.

# IT'S OUR RESPONSIBILITY TO NURTURE OUR RELATIONSHIP WITH NATURE

# WE
# ARE

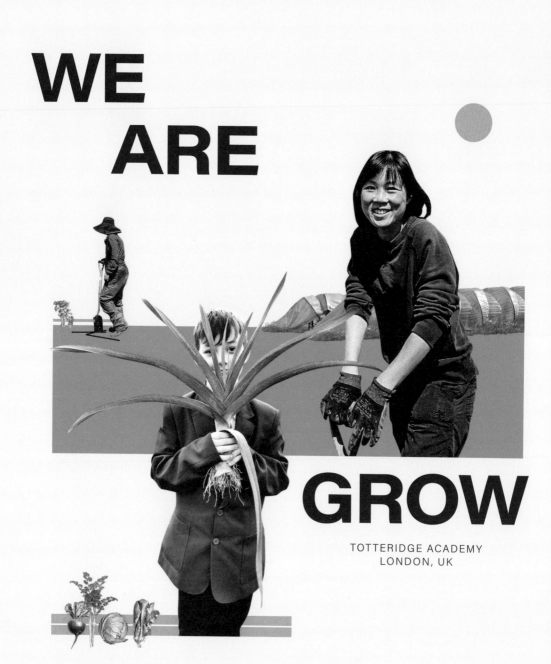

# GROW

TOTTERIDGE ACADEMY
LONDON, UK

GROW, embedded at The Totteridge Academy in North London, has brought life into the curriculum and community surrounding the school as it pilots and delivers programs that pivot on food growing and sustainable living. Because of the enthusiasm of the staff at The Totteridge Academy and the school's willingness to be open, flexible, and radical in its approach, GROW has developed a connection with students and the community, which has led to the development of a community farm built within the grounds of the school. This has proved to be a key asset in creating access to nature-based learning, and it has become a hub for extracurricular engagement—extending the reach beyond the walls of the school.

As well as providing the young people and the community with a much-needed resource to learn from and engage with their natural environment, GROW has been piloting models that make this charity commercially viable and self-sustaining. Although initially it relied heavily on funding and grants to develop and achieve its mission, which is a reality of many third-sector entities, its community farm now generates an income that also benefits the community and the environment using agroecological methods and practices (see Did You Know?, right). GROW's commitments include: protecting wildlife and biodiversity; providing access to vegetables that you don't see in the supermarkets so people can eat healthy, tasty food; fighting for food justice; being part of the local community; and supporting the need for fairly paid jobs in the local area.

## DID YOU KNOW?
—

Agroecology is sustainable farming that works with nature. Ecology is the study of relationships between plants, animals, people, and their environment— as well as the balance between these relationships. Thus, agroecology is the application of ecological concepts and principles in farming. It promotes farming practices that:

- mitigate climate change— reducing emissions, recycling resources, and prioritizing local supply chains
- work with wildlife— managing the impact of farming on wildlife and harnessing nature to do some of the hard work, like pollinating crops and controlling pests
- put farmers and communities in the driver's seat—giving power to local people and sustainable agricultural techniques

## WHAT CAN YOU DO?

It always helps when passionate and enthusiastic champions of learning, education, and the environment come together to create change on a vast scale, just like the collaboration between The Totteridge Academy and GROW, and there are things that we can take away from this to make small changes and steps in the right direction.

Try to understand where your food comes from and the carbon footprint of farm-to-table. Also, make conscious decisions on how and where you buy your food and, if you can, get your food locally and seasonally, while being conscious that such decisions are a luxury that not everyone can afford. It is important to note that people who can't make climate-conscious decisions should not be made to feel guilty. This is very much a luxury.

If you can, grow your own food, which could help you make savings as well as enjoy truly local produce. See the tips opposite.

Schools are where future generations start to lay the foundations for what they want to do with the rest of their lives and that is why it is so important to spotlight the importance of their local environment and what these children might be able to do to feed into that. It would be a missed opportunity if schools didn't become the access points and windows into nature-based education as part of the mainstream curriculum. Let's see schools as the heart of the community, where we plant seeds of change for the future.

Why not begin now, if you're a student, by asking your school if you can be allocated space in which to grow food to use in school lunches. If you're a teacher or administrator, say yes!

# LET'S START SEEING SCHOOLS AS THE HEART OF THE COMMUNITY, WHERE WE PLANT SEEDS OF CHANGE FOR THE FUTURE

## TIPS FOR YOUR NEW GARDENING SPACE

—

○ You can't go wrong by growing at home—plant microgreens and herbs like basil or chives on your windowsill to add flavor to your meals.

○ There's food to grow in every type of light: Swiss chard and beets tolerate shade while fruiting plants such as tomatoes, peppers, and cucumbers respond best to full sun.

○ Consider what growing space different crops need. For example, carrots require good soil depth, so would be best planted into the ground, whereas snow peas and snap peas will climb, making use of vertical spaces.

## DID YOU KNOW?

—

Food and farming are responsible for around 35 percent of global greenhouse gases, so reduce your carbon footprint and help combat climate change by growing some of your food.

# ROOT WINDOW PLANTER

**DID YOU KNOW?**

—

Mycorrhizal networks are found underground; they are created by the hyphae (filaments) of mycorrhizal fungi, which join with plant roots. Such networks connect individual plants and transfer water, carbon, nitrogen, and other nutrients and minerals between participants.

Reconnecting with nature is like a lifetime Netflix subscription but with no end and no fee. There is so much to discover, observe, and explore. One way to enhance your appreciation of nature's workings is by studying the very important processes going on within the soil layers. Surprisingly, there is considerable activity beneath the ground that we never get to see. Worms and ants are soil engineers, and they are crucial to the soil's ecosystem—breaking down the soil by eating organic matter and transforming it into smaller pieces.

Constructing a planter with a root window not only provides growing space but also allows you to study the fascinating underground processes. First you need to find a suitable space—depending on how big you want your planter or raised bed to be. Then measure length, width, and depth of your chosen site carefully. To follow this exact project, see pp.34–35 for the materials list and step-by-step instructions. If you cannot find decking in the sizes we have used, you can adjust the frame sizes as long as they are a multiple of a decking board width.

❯ The root window planter is great for small hands and curious minds, to get "behind the scenes" of gardening.

## YOU WILL NEED
—

- O  Measuring tape
- O  Pencil or pen
- O  Carpenter's try square
- O  Circular power saw or
  handsaw
- O  Combi drill driver
- O  $\frac{1}{6}$in (4mm) wood drill bit
- O  Screwdriver bits for combi
  drill driver
- O  6mm strong, transparent
  plastic (e.g. Perspex),
  $18\frac{3}{4}$×$13\frac{3}{4}$in (475×350mm)
- O  Weed barrier, 33ft (10m)
  long, 3ft (1m) wide
- O  Heavy duty staple gun,
  with heavy-duty staples,
  $\frac{1}{3}$in (8mm)
- O  Multipurpose potting mix
- O  Plants, to fit the planter

**Screws**
- O  exterior-grade,
  4mm timber screws,
  1in (30mm) long
- O  exterior-grade, 4mm timber
  screws, $1\frac{1}{2}$in (40mm) long
- O  exterior-grade, 4.5mm
  timber screws, $2\frac{1}{2}$in
  (60mm) long
- O  exterior-grade, 5mm timber
  screws, 3in (80mm) long

**Timber**
- O  4 pieces, $10\frac{3}{4}$in (274mm)
  long, of treated timber,
  $1\frac{1}{2}$×$1\frac{1}{2}$in (38×38mm), for
  the frame uprights
- O  4 pieces, $18\frac{3}{4}$in (475mm)
  long, of treated timber,
  $1\frac{1}{2}$×$1\frac{1}{2}$in (38×38mm), for
  the frame horizontals
- O  4 pieces, 11in (278mm)
  long, of treated timber,
  $1\frac{1}{2}$×$1\frac{1}{2}$in (38×38mm),
  for the rails
- O  8 panels, $13\frac{3}{4}$in (350mm)
  long, of decking board,
  $3\frac{3}{4}$×$3\frac{3}{4}$in (95×20mm), for
  the sides
- O  5 panels, $13\frac{3}{4}$in (350mm)
  long, of decking board,
  $3\frac{3}{4}$×$3\frac{3}{4}$in (95×20mm), for
  the back
- O  4 panels, $20\frac{1}{4}$in (515mm)
  long, of decking board,
  $3\frac{3}{4}$×$3\frac{3}{4}$in (95×20mm), for
  the base
- O  2 panels, $22\frac{3}{4}$in (578mm)
  long, of decking board,
  $3\frac{3}{4}$×$3\frac{3}{4}$in (95×20mm), for
  the long capping
- O  2 panels, $9\frac{1}{2}$in (242mm)
  long, of decking board,
  $3\frac{3}{4}$×$3\frac{3}{4}$in (95×20mm), for
  the short capping
- O  2 pieces, $13\frac{3}{4}$in (350mm)
  long, of treated timber,
  $1\frac{1}{2}$×$1\frac{1}{2}$in (38×38mm), for
  the feet

## HEALTH AND SAFETY
—

Gloves, ear protectors, and
eye protection is recommended
when cutting and drilling
into wood.

### 01

Cut each piece of timber and the plastic to size, having measured and marked it with the measuring tape and a pen or pencil, and having used the try square as a guide when cutting each piece with the saw.

### 02

To make the front and rear frames, drill pilot holes using the 4 mm drill bit at each end of every frame horizontal piece.

### 03

Using 2½-in (60-mm) screws, fix the frame horizontals to the frame uprights to make a frame. Each frame should be 18¾x13¾in (475x350 mm), the same size as the transparent plastic.

### 04

Align the plastic with one of the frames. Then drill pilot holes through the corners and edges of the plastic along the centerline of the timber, before using 1-in (30-mm) screws to affix to the wood. Next drill two pilot holes that go through the plastic and timber in each corner, on either side of the screws to form a diagonal line.

### 05

To join the two frames together, drill pilot holes in the corners of the open frame, then attach the four rails with the 3-in (80-mm) screws. Then place the transparent plastic and frame onto the ends of the rails so the plastic is on the inside of the box, and fix in place with the 3-in (80-mm) screws using the pilot holes created in step 04.

### 06

For the side and back panels, predrill into each corner of the panels, then affix to the frame using the 1½-in (40-mm) screws. Add the base panels so they line up with the vertical side panels, again using 1½-in (40-mm) screws to secure to the frame.

## 07

Predrill and screw the capping pieces into the top of the frame, with 1½-in (40-mm), so the inside edge of each capping piece is aligned with the inside face of the top of the frame. This allows for maximum planting area. The capping pieces should overhang the vertical faces of the planter by approximately 1¼-in (30-mm).

## 08

Predrill and screw the feet onto the bottom of the planter, using 2½-in (60-mm) screws.

## 09

Line the inside with weed barrier, stapling at high and low level to keep the barrier tight against the inside faces of the planter.

## 10

Fill with the compost and plants (for more planting information, see p.166). Do not lift from the capping pieces, which are held in only with screws. Always ask a friend to help move the planter from the base.

# ASAASE

JOSHUA KWAKU ASIEDU
ACCRA, GHANA

# LIVE TO LEARN

# LEARN TO LIVE

This project really epitomizes and emphasizes the need to revert back to what was—and it does so quite openly, too. In the words of Joshua Kwaku Asiedu, "The concept is nothing new; it is contrary really. Ancient and Indigenous cultures still teach us lessons today—[and are] often embedded and responsible for some of the biggest developments and innovations." Being self-sufficient might seem overwhelming in a world in which supermarkets and online streaming platforms offer infinite choice, quick access, and instant gratification, but Joshua has taken steps to do so and, subsequently, he is one of the biggest advocates of being at one with nature since he has journeyed back to his roots, both in heritage and beneath the ground.

Being born to a south Italian mother meant that the Italian way of life was pretty much all Joshua had known during his childhood, even though he has an Akuapim Ghanaian father. But after a seven year journey of personal growth and reconnection with the natural world that led him to the different environments of Australia, the US, India, New Zealand, Samoa, Japan, South Africa, and Ethiopia (to name a few), Joshua moved to Ghana, where he immersed himself in the local community and lived off the land his Ghanaian ancestors called home.

There he understood more about his Ghanaian ancestry as he familiarized himself not only with its rich history, his family ties, and the paths that they once walked, but also with the ecology of the very space he inherited from his family. Everything suddenly made sense to him. His destiny was for a life of adventure, exploration, and discovery—both inward and outward. He would settle in the land he would finally call home. What if existing, being present, and feeling fulfilled were the end goals? No fancy cars or lavish clothes could ever compete with the journey Joshua started to embark on. It was a feeling, a connection, a learning.

In a space immersed in the subtropical jungle of Ghana, West Africa, Joshua started to live off

# THE PROJECT IS CENTERED AROUND SUSTAINABLE LIVING IN DIRECT CONNECTION TO NATURE—MOTHER EARTH. IT IS THE DIRECT NURTURER OF HUMANITY, EARTH—OR AS WE CALL HER HERE—ASAASE YAA.

**JOSHUA KWAKU ASIEDU**

the land, growing his own food and using natural materials to make things such as dyes, paints, oils, and fertilizers. For him, everything now comes from the earth. He also built a metaphorical bridge, both in person and online, to awaken the masses to the possibilities and, more importantly, to the benefits of being at one with nature. While admitting that a lot of what he doing was experimental, he turned to the local masters who had continued practices of ancient knowledge.

Through programs and workshops, Joshua opened up his doors to welcome anyone into his sacred space to learn, connect, and love. In this way, he ensures that each one of us understands their place in the circle of life, and that they are equal to (not superior to) nature.

## WHAT CAN YOU DO?

Not everyone has the luxury of making such a trip to beautiful Ghana. However, there are a few things you can do at home to reconnect with nature: use natural dyes such as beets, blackberries, or rhubarb root to repurpose or recolor some clothing; make natural essential oils with plants, for example, from basil, lavender, or marigold (*Calendula*), to put in food, on your skin, or in your hair; and create your own new plants by placing a stem in a jar of water until it has developed roots and can then be planted in soil (this method works really well using mint). See opposite for two of Joshua's recipes for natural paint and oil.

## AVOCADO OIL

—

O  Cut an avocado in half
   and remove the seed
   and skin.
O  Mash the pulp in a bowl
   until smooth.
O  Spread the mashed avocado
   on a flat tray and allow to
   dry out for a few days.
O  Place the dried mash in
   a piece of upcycled
   cheesecloth and squeeze
   it over a bowl, to
   extract the oil.
O  Bottle up the avocado oil
   in an upcycled, sealable
   oil bottle.
O  Use the avocado oil in
   foods, on your skin, or in
   your hair.

## BROWN NATURAL PAINT

—

O  Collect a sizable bowl of
   sand (for consistency) and
   a separate bowl of clay
   (for pigmentation) and
   allow both materials
   to dry.
O  Slice a banana (for use as
   a binder) and allow to dry
   on a tray.
O  Pound each of these dried
   materials separately, then
   sift each so it's a fine
   powder.
O  Mix the sand and clay
   powders together and add
   water to create a paste.
O  Separately, add cold water
   to the banana flour to make
   a paste. Then boil some
   water in a pan and add the
   boiling water to your
   banana flour paste. Mix and
   allow to cool.
O  Combine the sand and clay
   paste with the banana
   flour paste. Mix
   thoroughly.

# KEYHOLE RAISED BED

## YOU WILL NEED
—

(for a bed 84 in/220 cm diameter and 17½ in/44 cm tall)

- Spade, forks, shovel
- String, small stones, or sand, for marking the edge around the keyhole bed
- Wooden stake with a piece of string that is slightly longer than the half the plot size
- 28 hollow concrete blocks, 17½×8¾×8¾ in (440×220×220 mm)
- Gravel for drainage within the bed
- Soil
- Plants for keyhole garden
- Compost materials for compost bin
- Container with holes in its sides such as the 40-gallon (180-liter) anti-root spiral planter

Nothing we do, create, or invent is truly new. We tend to claim ideas and put our name to them and, subsequently, dismiss and disrespect the historic and cultural roots that would teach us so much about ourselves and the planet that we call home. The passing down of lessons and stories offers us context to our lives, whether it is art, architecture, mathematics, agriculture, or horticulture.

The keyhole garden, which channels ancient, agricultural, cyclical techniques originating in Africa, was spotlighted in the 1990s as a way to solve very drought-ridden and otherwise infertile small spaces on which families might grow their own food. By building up the soil in such a place with a retaining wall—logs, bricks, or even stones—it was possible to create a nutrient-rich growing space, and a self-sustaining system through a central composting cage.

Keyhole gardening is something anyone can do, using the most basic of materials found anywhere. It is the perfect low-maintenance, small-space solution to meet the wish to grow food and it also establishes a mini ecosystem in the wildlife-friendly way it is built. It can be adapted to any shape and size, with no need for drills or screws, and it even boasts a self-fertilizing compost system in the middle.

Find an appropriate site, ensuring you have enough space for the keyhole garden as well as easy access to it. Clear and level the site, ensuring there is no more than 2 in (5 cm) between the highest and lowest points. Also think about the materials that will be needed to build your retaining garden wall—we've chosen cinder blocks for this project, but you may prefer to use wood or brick.

## 01

Clear and level the space. Then pinpoint the center of your chosen area and use a string, sand, or small stones to mark an outer circle to guide where you'll be building the retaining garden wall.

## 02

Mark another smaller circle in the center (use the container with holes in its sides as a guide); this is where the fresh composting material will be placed.

## 03

Start to erect the first layer of the retaining wall (here, of cinder blocks) following the string, sand, or stone outline as closely as possible. Ensure the corners of the blocks touch each other so there aren't large gaps.

## 04

Once you've done the first layer, the second one is offset by half a cinder block. (In a similar way to building a brick wall, this overlapping method creates stability in your structure.) Continue building in this way until you have reached the required height for your keyhole garden.

## 05

Place the container in the marked central compost circle. Now that your compost bin is in place and the outer retaining wall has been built, fill the space between them with a base layer of gravel, top up with soil, and plant the bed. Then start to fill your central bin with composting material (see p.063).

# REGENERATE

/rɪˈdʒen.ə.reɪt/

**Regenerate**
*Verb*
to re-create, renew, or invigorate;
and improve upon a place or system

# WE MUST PRESS

# THE RESET BUTTON

How have we got to a point where much of our lives are pulled, dragged, and dictated by greed, power, and profit? We need to consider what's better, and for whom. What has happened to respect, connection, feeling, empathy, understanding? All of these are free, costing absolutely nothing, and should undeniably be given a lot more thought before pushing forward with agendas, motives, and plans to scale up and expand. The obsession with profit comes at the expense of the planet we live on. It's crazy how the word "growth" has been hijacked by economics—what about growth in ecology or psychology? We have used and abused our home and our surroundings, disregarding and, at times, choosing to ignore the consequences of any irresponsible actions.

I use the word "growth" carefully as I know there are many that care dearly for what the future holds. We take for granted the riches of our natural resources, viewing them as assets rather than as part of a process—a bigger picture. We impose a value on them as part of this transactional culture for our selfish and often unnecessary use, instead of understanding the role they play in our ecological landscape. Surely the very fact that our natural resources are so difficult to access should have been a warning not to take them.

I'd be completely dishonest if I didn't acknowledge the part I play in this way of life,

which I vehemently oppose. I've come to realize that it's okay to not be perfect, but we have to at least take steps to improve the situation.

The world is in desperate need of rehabilitation. With rates of extraction and depletion going way beyond the point of balance, we need to think about how we can accelerate the rate of regeneration. To my mind, there are two options. One is that all 7.84 billion people vacate the planet at once—allowing the planet the time and space it needs to heal, restore, and revive itself organically, naturally, and without hesitation—but I have a feeling that people are not going anywhere. The other—and preferable—option is to support, enable, and accelerate the regenerative processes that would otherwise occur if we had no say in the matter.

We must press the reset button.

## THE SOIL-UTION

The solutions are out there—even right beneath our feet, soil is full of opportunities. Soil is what feeds us, nurtures us, and is the foundation for us to walk, build, and exist on. That's why it's so important that we, as consumers, understand the journey and processes behind food production.

Admittedly, to have the capacity to think about it, let alone take action on it, is a luxury.

# THE WORD "GROWTH" HAS BEEN HIJACKED BY ECONOMICS—WHAT ABOUT GROWTH IN ECOLOGY?

Organic foods are often beyond the price range of many—we have to acknowledge that some people are living on the breadline and are being forced to choose between heating and eating. The food industry requires remodeling; the mission has to change; the scope needs to think about the bigger picture—the long term. Allow me to introduce regenerative agriculture, which is being adopted more and more by the agricultural industry.

## REGENERATIVE AGRICULTURE

This seeks to transform the current unsustainable farming practices by ensuring that the needs of plants, people, and wildlife within the wider environment have equal priority when food is produced commercially. This can be done by following these five basic principles:

> Limiting tilling the soil—or avoiding it completely—so physical, biological, and chemical disturbances are minimized.
> Keeping soil covered with vegetation and natural materials by mulching, using ground cover crops, and sowing pasture lands.
> Building healthy soils, which retain excess water and nutrients, by increasing plant diversity, and thereby also benefiting wildlife and pollinators.

> Keeping living roots in the soil as much as possible—to help stabilize it—by not clearing spent crops, by planting winter cover crops, or by having land in permanent pasture.
> Using animal manure as much as possible to feed the soil and to capture carbon and water. This will also reduce polluted runoff and the need for artificial fertilizers.

See my conversation with George Lamb, cofounder of Wildfarmed, on pp.050–051 to find out more about regenerative agriculture.

## THE MUSHROOM MOVEMENT

Mushrooms are a type of fungus and are often enjoyed as food available in plastic packaging from supermarket shelves; other types of fungus such as toadstools are generally poisonous, magical, or untouchable. However, all fungi offer so much more than these descriptions. By understanding their functions, we can begin to respect, appreciate, and protect the way in which they grow. The benefits are endless— here are just a few.

## SOIL NUTRITION

Fungi are integral to the way plants receive and access nutrients in the soil. Some fungi decompose plant and animal debris, recycling the availability of nutrients in the soil. They can also store nitrogen and make phosphorus available in the soil; these are two of the main nutrients required for plant development and productivity. Fungi transfer these nutrients via the mycorrhizal network underground, connecting individual plants together and enabling the exchange of nutrients.

## REDUCTION IN WASTE

Edible mushrooms can be grown using agricultural waste, which means they don't need fertile soil like other crops. Therefore, mushroom cultivation can reuse agro-waste while increasing food supply.

## CARBON STORE AND PROTECTION FROM POLLUTANTS

Not only do fungi support plants, but plants support fungi, too. Fungi rely on carbon captured by the plants, which they access via plant roots and store in the soil. As decomposers, fungi also remove carbon from organic matter. These processes not only store carbon but also improve soil fertility.

Research has also found that fungi have the ability to degrade pollutants, such as oil and plastic—petroleum-based products that are often found in pharmaceuticals and personal care products. Such substances accumulate in the environment and take a long time to break down.

## DID YOU KNOW?

—

One teaspoon of soil contains more living organisms than there are people in the world. The biological diversity in the soil, although often overlooked, is crucial to life on Earth itself—without such organisms, there would be no terrestrial life.

## SUSTAINABLE MATERIALS

The mushroom root system, mycelium, is now being used as a sustainable alternative to synthetic, plastic, and animal-based products. Mycelium products use fewer land and water resources to make and are biodegradable. Some shoes, clothes, packaging, and skincare products are already made using mycelium.

## HUMAN HEALTH

Edible mushrooms are rich in nutrients (such as vitamins B, C, and D), fiber, protein, and minerals (including potassium, phosphorus, and calcium). Due to their protein content, edible mushrooms are a good meat substitute in plant-based diets. Plus, did you know that 6 percent of edible mushrooms possess medicinal properties? They have the capability to prevent diseases and boost immune systems. Shiitake is one example: this mushroom has antiviral properties and can reduce serum cholesterol, too. Other species possess antioxidants, reduce blood pressure, and combat the effects of diabetes.

## In conversation with
## GEORGE LAMB

George Lamb set up education initiative, GROW, working with schools, before cofounding Wildfarmed—a network of farmers embracing soil-focused farming.

**TAYSHAN What does regenerative agriculture mean to you?**

**GEORGE** I've been involved in it now for the best part of 10 years. Unfortunately, the conventional farming system, which accounts for 98 percent of Britain's agriculture, is all based around chemicals, rather than biology. Ultimately, regenerative agriculture is about getting life back into the field. If your fields are full of life, then your food is going to be full of life. Our guiding principle is you can't use any 'cides (pesticides, herbicides, fungicides). If you think about homicide, suicide—'cides is a Latin word for death and you don't want any death added to your field. So Wildfarmed doesn't use any 'cides. Regenerative agriculture is basically just ancient wisdom, but figuring out how we can make it more efficient for the 21st century. In practical terms, it's making sure you're not using any 'cides and you encourage biodiversity. It's about mimicking nature, and you don't get monocrops in nature. So if you look at one of our fields, you'll see a minimum of two plant groups there—that's called bi-cropping. And we also do a lot of polycropping where you might have three or four in there. Dr. Christine Jones, who's one of the principal soil scientists in the world, recommends growing plants from at least four different plant families in close proximity. The diversity of plant root exudates stimulates soil biological activity, enhancing nutrient uptake, carbon sequestration, and disease protection.

**TAYSHAN And how do we get that message across, because it's not just business, it's trying to heal the planet and bring everyone together on the same page?**

**GEORGE** I think anything you can do to reconnect people with nature is a step in the right direction. Particularly people who live in cities have lost touch with the food supply. I remember one kid at a school that I was working with asking, "where do potatoes come from? the freezer?" And it's fair, they do come from the freezer. But there were some steps before that. So, I think anything we can do to make the bond between the consumer and the farmer stronger has got to be a positive. You know, if you're living in the city, your only definite opportunity to connect with nature is when you eat a couple of times a day. You might get some time in the park. You might go past the trees, but a couple of times a day, you're putting stuff in your mouth that's been grown.

**TAYSHAN But you're not really thinking "where's it from?" So it's about trying to put it at the forefront of people's minds. Do you feel like people are listening?**

**GEORGE** People don't like change and we're all guilty of it. So if I tell you I'd like you to farm in a different way to how you've done it your entire adult life, you might be resistant to that. But we've got to a point where we've squeezed farmers as much as we can. 50 years ago in the US, 70 cents to the dollar was going to the farmer, now it's 10 cents. All the risk sits with the farmer, none of it sits with the food suppliers. So you've got these farmers locked in the chemical agriculture system and then you ask "why don't we try something different?"

**TAYSHAN Slightly different question. What would you call yourself in this space?**

**GEORGE** Chief amplifier, basically. I'm a connector of people. I'm a starter motor. I believe in this thing 1,000,000 percent.

**TAYSHAN I think that's where we resonate. The RHS Chelsea Flower Show garden that we did this year was called Closing the Green Gap, highlighting the inequality in access to green space. Growing up in Ladbroke Grove, you've got a massive divide in wealth and access. You will find the organic health shops on one side of the borough and all the chicken shops on the other side. Within a 10 minute walk, the average life expectancy differs by 17 years. So how do we create access to healthy, organic foods?**

**GEORGE** Ultimately, it all comes down to education. We haven't prioritized health and nutrition. And unfortunately, we find ourselves in a situation where the only metric of value is essentially accumulation of wealth or our ability to exhibit it through material objects. The irony is that you will poison yourself, you will forgo health in order to exhibit wealth, or your perception of wealth.

**TAYSHAN Access is resources and knowledge. And education can shift mindset. It's all about sparking something in people. It's important for people to believe and feel part of the movement. I see it more as a movement than anything else.**

# HOMEACRES

CHARLES DOWDING
SOMERSET, UK

I've been an avid follower of Charles Dowding for quite some years, after stumbling into horticulture in 2017. I'd spend many late nights watching his YouTube videos with an enthusiasm to learn and understand as much as I could about a no-dig approach to agriculture and horticulture.

Fast forward a few years and I've been fortunate enough to have met Charles a handful of times now—on one occasion he hosted myself and my family at Homeacres, his home in Somerset, where he grows and films his videos.

Charles is most well-known as an advocate for the no-dig gardening method—it really is as simple as it sounds (see more detail on the next page). Yet, it's easy to overlook just how radical and how bold Charles has been in raising environmental awareness. Although it's only quite recently that his no-dig methods have caught the attention of hundreds of thousands online, with

Charles amassing more than 600,000 subscribers on YouTube, his understanding of the relationship between gardening and the environment began in 1979, when he started to ask some very important questions of the agricultural industry and its exploitative ways as he explored and experimented on his own land. As with pretty much everything that exists, nothing is new: Charles has been influenced and inspired by earlier no-dig advocates Arthur Guest, F. C. King, and William Shewell-Cooper, and he has tuned into their ideologies and methods. However, it is so important for us to realize that no-dig gardening has been around for centuries—with many cultures planting in relatively undisturbed soils and not digging their fields. Such an approach is still embedded in their way of life.

# MANY CULTURES PLANT IN RELATIVELY UNDISTURBED SOILS AND DO NOT DIG THEIR FIELDS

## NO-DIG PRINCIPLES

The great advantage of the no-dig approach to growing food is that it requires less effort and yet provides higher yields. There are two main aspects to bear in mind: keep soil disturbances to a minimum; and feed the soil.

The ecosystem within the soil is what will retain the soil structure and ensure its content is as rich as can be. To help this process, the soil needs plenty of biological activity. The best way to enable this is by spreading compost on the surface. You can make your own with green and brown waste materials (see p.063), buy peat-free potting mix, or even use local horse manure.

## WHAT CAN YOU DO?

The no-dig approach to growing plants is about enhancing the ecosystem through circular soil systems, too. You could, therefore, start to think about how what you grow can, eventually, go back into the ground, feed the soil, and bring more life in the most natural, least disruptive way possible. Then go on to set up your own composting system (see pp.056–0.63) using organic matter from your kitchen and outdoor areas. Such composting of waste materials can be done in many ways: from a small, portable compost bin on a balcony up to a multi-segmented composting system, which requires turning over at regular intervals.

Another thing that we should celebrate is our ability to steer and guide the ecology to an extent that no other species can. With no-dig, there's a strategy—a plan—that's well thought through. So I ask the question, "How could you integrate no-dig into your growing journey?"

(see pp.056–0.63)

## NO-DIG METHOD
—

### 01

Having identified a suitable plot for your no-dig garden—this could be on an existing lawn, in soil, or even over concrete—cover the space with cardboard to suppress and kill off any weeds in your chosen space. The decomposing weeds will add to the nutrients in the soil, and the cardboard will break down and disintegrate into the soil over time.

### 02

Add a thick layer of well-rotted compost to the plot—still no digging involved!

### 03

With your hands, plant your crops in the layer of compost. Always ensure you water in the plants very well. Then enjoy the abundance of food from your no-dig garden. Keep an eye out for weeds growing back— such as ground elder (*Aegopodium podagraria*), couch grass (*Elymus repens*), and bindweed (*Convolvulus*)— and pull out any you see.

# COMPOST BIN
# AND COMPOSTING

This compost bin will provide the much-needed space to celebrate the benefits of what happens beneath the surface. We often celebrate the flowers or fruits that parade color and vibrancy—but what about the soil? Credit where credit's due, and it's the soil where all the magic happens. If you've been wondering all this time where you might be able to put your excess food waste, or leaves that have fallen from trees and shrubs, or even pruned plant waste—here is exactly what you can do to turn waste into a resource.

Compost is at the crux of all things in the garden. It should be treated as gold dust, as it gives life to anything it touches—quite literally. Thus, it really does feel like an injustice calling the container for such a rich, valuable, and integral part of our existence a "mere" bin. Filling a compost bin doesn't need to feel as if it's a chore or an extra job on the to-do list, despite a few gardeners viewing it as a smelly and slimy necessity.

To build a bin in your space, clear an area in the garden where the ground is level to within 2 in (5 cm) of the highest and lowest points. If the bin is to be positioned on earth, then level out the surface with gardening tools (rake, spade, shovel etc.). Measure your space to figure out how large your compost bin can be, and if you have space to incorporate multiple bins. A good-size bin is roughly 100x32x32 in (1x0.8x0.8 m).

→ Having more than one bin allows you to turn over material from one bin to another, thereby accelerating the composting process.

**COMPOST SHOULD BE TREATED AS GOLD DUST, AS IT GIVES LIFE TO ANYTHING IT TOUCHES**

## YOU WILL NEED
—

for two connected bins,
84×32×32 in/2.2×0.8×0.8 m

- O Spade, forks, shovel for
  site leveling (if needed)
- O Measuring tape
- O Carpenter's try square
- O Pencil or pen
- O Circular power saw or
  handsaw
- O Combi drill driver
- O $^1\!/_6$-in (4-mm) drill bit,
  suitable for timber
- O Screwdriver bits for combi
  drill driver
- O Chicken wire mesh, 3 ft
  (1m) wide and 33 ft (10m)
  long
- O Wire staples, $^1\!/_{10}$-in
  (2.7-mm) diameter and 1-in
  (25-mm) high
- O Wire cutters

### Screws

- O exterior-grade, 4mm timber
  screws, 1$^1\!/_2$ in (40mm) long
- O exterior-grade, 4.5mm
  timber screws, 3 in (80mm)
  long

## HEALTH AND SAFETY
—

In addition to the materials
list below, when cutting and
drilling timber you should
always wear gloves, safety
goggles for eye protection,
and ear protectors.

### Timber

- O 12 panels, 31 in (800mm)
  long, of decking board,
  4$^3\!/_4$×$^3\!/_4$ in (120×20mm), for
  the sides
- O 3 panels, 7$^1\!/_3$ in (2.2m)
  long, of decking board,
  4$^3\!/_4$×$^3\!/_4$ in (120×20mm), for
  the back
- O 10 corner posts, 31 in
  (800mm) long, of treated
  timber, 1$^3\!/_8$×2$^1\!/_2$ in (35×60mm)
- O 8 spacers, 9$^1\!/_2$ in (240mm)
  long, of decking board
  offcuts,* 2$^1\!/_2$×$^3\!/_4$ in
  (60×20mm) (optional)
- O 12 panels, 38 in (980mm)
  long, of decking board,
  4$^3\!/_4$×$^3\!/_4$ in (120×20mm), for
  the front (optional)
- O 4 battens, 31 in (800mm)
  long, of treated timber,
  13$^3\!/_8$×2$^1\!/_2$ in (35×60mm)
  (optional)

\* A decking board offcut split
  down the center

## 01

Measure all your wood pieces to size, using the tape measure and try square, and a pencil or pen.

## 02

Use the try square to indicate where to make the cut along the markings. Cut the marked wood with the saw.

## 03

To create a wall, you need three side panels and two corner posts. Lay them out so the three panels run equidistantly across the two posts. Mark halfway across both posts to line up the middle panel. Drill pilot holes into each corner of the panels in line with the center line of the posts. Using the 1½-in (40-mm) screws, drill one screw on the inside edge of each side panel on both posts.

## 04

Measure the diagonal in both directions. If the measure is the same it will be square. If not, you can realign the panels. Once it's perfectly square, screw the outside edge at both ends on all four panels.

## 05

Repeat steps 03–04 to make the second wall. If you're building multi-bins, like we did, you will need three walls—one will join two bins in the middle. Once you've made three walls, turn one over and follow steps 03–05 again to add three more panels to the other side. This will be the middle wall.

## 06

To fix the back panels, stand the walls on the post edge with the panels upright and equidistant, and place the back panels across the top, middle, and bottom, evenly spaced. With the 3-in (80-mm) screws, fix the back panel into the wall posts.

07

Decking boards usually come in widths of 4³⁄₄ in (120 mm), 4⁷⁄₈ in (125 mm), or 5 in (150 mm) and lengths of 7³⁄₄ ft (2.4 m) or 11¹⁄₂ ft (3.6 m). We chose 7³⁄₄-ft (2.4-m) lengths because this is what fit into our vehicle. If you can get wood delivered for the project, then 11¹⁄₂-ft (3.6-m) lengths might offer more opportunities to save wood and money. However, going to the store yourself to choose pieces helps avoid bananas (bent, warped, or twisted boards). You can also select nice-looking boards this way. They should have been tanalized and pressure-treated and so are resistant to the weather and bugs. However, if they are continuously left moist/sodden, they will eventually rot away—that is why we use linings in our compost bins.

## 07

Position the entire assembly into place. Tightly wrap chicken wire around the inside, and fold around the front posts. As you go, hammer in wire staples to secure the wire in place. You may need someone to help you.

## 08

Use the remaining post pieces to create front caps to cover the chicken wire and position these slightly to the inside to create a lip, using the 3-in (80-mm) screws. You'll need one post at each end and two in the middle if adjoining bins. Screw in place at the top and bottom. Then tidy the chicken wire with the wire cutters. If you wish to add front panels for tidiness, follow steps 09–11.

08

## 09

Using the 1½-in (40-mm) screws, fix a spacer vertically on the front post of each wall in the gap between the horizontal panels. Place a front panel on the inside of each bin at the bottom, resting against the vertical capping pieces.

## 10

Screw the battens vertically onto the wall panels on each side, leaving a ⅛–¼-in (3–5-mm) gap so the front panels can be lifted through the channel.

## 11

Slot in the remaining front panels.

# HOW TO MAKE GARDEN COMPOST

A properly tended compost bin accelerates the rotting down of organic matter into invaluable, humus-rich garden compost. To make successful garden compost, you must put a balanced mixture of green and brown materials (see list, right) into the bin. It takes about three months in summer for the ingredients to decompose into garden compost, and longer at lower temperatures. Turning the ingredients helps speed up the process; ideally, this should be done every 2–3 weeks. If the weather is dry, add water to the decomposing matter to keep it moist. You will know when it is ready to use because fully mature garden compost is dark brown and sweet-smelling, with a crumbly texture.

## GREEN MATERIALS FOR COMPOSTING
—

- O   Vegetable peels
- O   Fruit scraps
- O   Coffee grounds
- O   Cut flowers
- O   Garden and house plants
- O   Young annual weeds
- O   Grass clippings

## BROWN MATERIALS FOR COMPOSTING
—

- O   Paper egg cartons
- O   Toilet paper tubes
- O   Paper towels
- O   Leaves
- O   Hedge clippings
- O   Shredded paper
- O   Scrunched-up newspaper
- O   Chopped, moist straw and hay

# GROW YOUR OWN

# MUSHROOMS

I came across Sal in the aftermath of the Grenfell Tower fire in an ideas-sharing gathering, where local people were invited to pitch ways in which the community could heal. With Sal's adoration for mushrooms, and my passion for gardening, we joined forces to bring nature, in all forms, to the people. Sal runs workshops in London, teaching people how they can easily grow mushrooms at home. You can cultivate them indoors or outdoors, and they don't require much room. Here, I show how to grow oyster mushrooms in a laundry basket indoors, as well as how to introduce a loggery of shiitake into an outdoor space. You can buy the mushroom spawn from a specialized supplier, or make your own using bought spores. To do so using a 1¾ pint (1 liter) sterilized jar, mix your mushroom spores with 9 oz (250 g) precooked grains (for example, brown rice, popcorn kernels, barley), then leave for 3–4 weeks in a dark place, at 68°F (20°C). The spawn is ready for use once it's turned white.

## IN A BASKET

### 01
Sterilize straw overnight in a bucket with lime powder and boiling water mixed at a ratio of ½oz per 1 pint (2g per 1 liter); then drain.

### 02
Clean the laundry basket thoroughly using high-grade alcohol. Add the sterilized, drained straw.

### 03
Mix the mushroom spawn into the straw at a ratio of 1:10.

### 04
Leave the basket in a sheltered place that never gets warmer than 72°F (22°C), for at least six weeks.

### 05
Use a spray bottle to mist the mushroom straw mix once a day until harvest, to avoid it drying out.

### 06
When the mushrooms have fully developed, they will be ready to harvest and be enjoyed.

### WARNING!
—

Only eat foraged mushrooms
that have been identified
by a guide or other
trusted expert.

## YOU WILL NEED
—

O  Straw
O  Bucket
O  Lime powder
O  Laundry basket
   with holes
O  High-grade
   alcohol
O  Pack of edible-
   mushroom spawn
O  Spray bottle

## LOGGERY

### 01
Find some freshly cut hardwood logs and drill holes along each log.

### 02
Hammer purchased plugs of shiitake mushroom spores into the holes. Then melt log sealing wax and cover the plugged holes with the wax.

### 03
Create a small pile of inoculated logs in an untouched, unused, usually shady spot.

### 04
Leave the logs to incubate for 18–24 months, allowing time for the mycelium to colonize the log. The mushrooms will then appear.

## YOU WILL NEED
—

O  Hardwood logs
O  Electric drill
   and drill bits
O  Pack of shiitake
   mushroom spores
O  Log sealing wax
O  Heat source to
   melt the wax
O  Paintbrush or
   sponge to apply
   the melted wax)

# MARUVAN

### AKIRA MIYAWAKI AND SUGI PROJECT
### RAJASTHAN, INDIA

The Miyawaki method, named after late, great, Japanese botanist Akira Miyawaki, is all about working with nature—looking at space through a native lens, embracing, harnessing, and improving the local ecology. This is done by planting wildlife-friendly, native woodland plants in a specially prepared small area of ground.

At a similar time to Charles Dowding (see p.052), throughout the 1970s, Miyawaki would observe the decline of natural forests in his homeland of Japan, which were once thriving with native trees. On his journey to understanding the changing landscape, he calculated that only 0.06 percent of contemporary Japanese forests were indigenous. Since then, Miyawaki has encouraged an international movement, with institutions, communities, and individuals adopting and taking inspiration from what initially started as an experiment, and bringing it forward into an increasingly mainstream space. One nonprofit organization that has done just that is SUGi, which finances afforestation projects.

**DID YOU KNOW?**
—

SUGi has delivered 175 afforestation projects in 27 countries and 40 cities worldwide—restoring a total 1,633,434 sq ft (151,751 sq m). In the process, 306,282 native trees have been planted, restoring 785 species with a tree survival rate of 89 percent. In doing so, SUGi has impacted the lives of 40,000 young people, educating them on the value of pocket forests for communities and the environment.

# RAJASTHAN, INDIA—MARUVAN

In the Maruvan project, SUGi set out to bring life back to the Thar Desert, a barren, ecologically void area in the northwestern part of the Indian subcontinent. (Maruvan means "Forest of the Desert.") Previously used as farmland, this project of ecological revival was based in Rajasthan, where most of the wide and inhospitable Thar Desert lies, and involved turning to the very methods that Akira Miyawaki had experimented with on the other side of Asia, in Japan.

With the help of a forest-creation company called Afforestt, 1,000 trees, comprising 46 native species, were densely planted in the space of 300 sq yd (250 sq m) to kick-start the mission to revive the local ecological systems of Rajasthan.

Since the first planting in November 2020, surveys and reports have shown just how much biodiversity has increased. Several species of snake; 16 species of birds; and several types of pollinators, such as bees, wasps, and various butterflies, have joined now-thriving species including Indian crested porcupine (*Hystrix indica*), Indian hedgehogs (*Paraechinus micropus*), desert fox (*Vulpes vulpes pusilla*), Indian gray mongoose (*Urva edwardsii*), black-naped hare (*Lepus nigricollis*), and Indian desert gerbil (*Meriones hurrianae*). The new trees have a survival rate of 91 percent, and the tallest one is now standing at more than 6½ ft (2 m).

Thus the legacy of Akira Miyawaki continues through the much-needed work of SUGi—touching corners of the world such as India, the UK, Brazil, South Africa, Cameroon, and the US.

Two years on from planting, the SUGi Pocket Forests are deemed to be self-sustaining, allowing nature to run its course and develop in whichever way it chooses.

## WHAT CAN YOU DO?

I'd urge you to think about your local space and what you might be able to do to support the ecology in your vicinity. It's so important that we also actively develop areas that seem to have no use or function for the human population, but are so vital to the very many species of plants and animals that we often overlook.

Seek projects that are already active in planting up local spaces. Frequently, the organizers have done their research and so bring layers of expertise, science, and design to the project. Although this is not a necessity, it is helpful to bringing on board a community of people, too.

You can also start small and plant a tree in your own space—if everyone did that we'd have 8 billion trees. See how to plant your own tree on the next page.

## IT'S SO IMPORTANT WE ACTIVELY DEVELOP AREAS THAT ARE SO VITAL FOR PLANTS AND ANIMALS

# PLANT A TREE IN A CONTAINER

## DID YOU KNOW?

—

Healthy urban trees are known to have a cooling benefit. They do this through the release of water vapor, in the process of evapotranspiration. Trees also provide cooling through the provision of shade and because they reflect more solar radiation and store less energy than many artificial surfaces such as concrete and asphalt.

Trees—both small and large—offer many benefits, and can be planted almost anywhere when grown in a container. Therefore, if you don't have an open green space or what is typically perceived as a "garden," don't let that limit your planting ideas. Why not grow a tree in a pot and match it with adjacent styles, colors, shapes, and textures to lift a small spot on your balcony, on your rooftop, or even in your living room (depending on the choice of tree).

Your choice of tree may bring fruit and flowers; it might take you to a different place or a memory; it might attract insects and create new ecosystems in its soil; it might have a good taste or smell, or be something you like to touch; its beauty might just bring you joy. My banana tree reminds me of the tropics of Jamaica—a country with a culture that has made its mark in Notting Hill, where I live.

Maybe name your tree to keep you company, and you could even put it on wheels so you can move it around. It could be wheeled about to create pockets of shade and maybe relocated to a permanent home in the ground one day.

## 01

Source a container that is three times as wide as the tree's root system and is slightly deeper than the distance between the base of the root ball and the nursery line mark, showing where the tree was previously planted. It must have a drainage hole in the bottom.

## 02

Soak the root ball in water.

## 03

Cover the bottom of the container with broken pottery and a layer of grit, for drainage. Then half fill with loam-based potting mix.

## 04

Loosen the tree roots to encourage growth. Then place the tree in the container. Backfill with potting mix, up to the height of the tree nursery line, leaving a gap between the nursery line and rim of the container so it can fill with water.

## 05

I have underplanted around the base of the tree with ferns, erigeron, and pennisetum grasses. Then lightly firm the potting mix and water well.

# REIMAGINE

/ˌriː.ɪˈmædʒ.ɪn/

# WAS IT ALL DONE BY

# ACCIDENT

# OR BY
# DESIGN?

**DID YOU KNOW?**

—

Eco-anxiety is the chronic
fear of environmental doom
that comes from watching
the slow and seemingly
irrevocable impacts of
climate change unfold, and
worrying about the future
for oneself, children, and
later generations (American
Psychological Association).

While the destiny of people and planet may seem daunting and overwhelming to say the least, the future of the world needs to be viewed as an exciting opportunity and a challenge to be creative, to seek solutions, and to be radical in our approach through design, education, and culture.

Quite simply, we must break free of the norms that have landed us where we are now and must widen our horizons to limitless and undiscovered possibilities. The convenience and comfort in routine and institution are lazy, careless, and regressive. "Because it's always been this way" is an answer I cannot stand and will no longer tolerate, and I don't think anyone else should, for that matter! The vision has drastically altered, yet the infrastructure to enable that change is nowhere near as established as it needs to be— whether it's governments who are ignoring the very obvious flaws in systems, models, and policies, or it's established institutions still operating with the same mission and scope put in place some hundred years ago.

It's sometimes easy, and completely understandable, to be consumed and intimidated by the very valid and urgent concerns and worries about the way we treat our planet and the consequences that are now impacting us all—it's no longer just theory. How we view space is very much dictated by the lens we choose to look through. Our everyday surroundings and experiences are affected by past decisions, and there is a balance to be found. The past produced works of beauty, innovation, and wonder—from the pyramids of Giza in Egypt, to the Taj Mahal in India, or Machu Picchu in Peru. It's important to celebrate and protect the past because it very much gives us context as to where we are now and the journey that we've been on as a people. Yet not all past decisions and designs hold that weight, and this is where change is essential.

I bring to your attention North Kensington, London—the area I'm most familiar with, but not always for the right reasons. I walk out of my door and what do I see—a couple of pubs; a betting shop; corner stores packed with sweets, chocolate, and alcohol; a few fast-food restaurants ... and what's left of Grenfell Tower. Is this what we must accept as our reality? Is this the life that was chosen for us? For our children? Was it all done by accident or by design?

■ **Accident**
☒ **Design**

I will always argue the latter. From the placement of trees, to housing and shops, "experts" once sat around a table and made decisions on our behalf—for better or for worse.

We need to start being at the table when it comes to design, seeing ourselves as creatives and taking ownership of the future of our locality. Every community has very intricate and bespoke needs—design should be more collaborative, more patient, and more understanding.

Consultation and engagement should be equally as important as the excitement of the technical design and construction process, because if you don't have the people on board you'll end up with a space that lacks function, use, and purpose. While there are no correct solutions or routes to go down, co-design needs to become the norm in public, community spaces—let's pilot how we engage, onboard, and sustain relationships within communities and with our natural surroundings. It's an amazing opportunity to optimize connection between residents, community, local authorities, designers, and developers. It needs to be cohesive and always mutually beneficial.

## WHAT IS CO-DESIGN?

Co-design harnesses the power of true collaboration—designing with and not for. It's realizing that communities, residents, and local stakeholders must play a part in the design process in which the outcome of a space improves their everyday experience. Just think about all the areas that have been designed without the insight, context, and local support that could so improve them. Co-design addresses the imbalance of power held by individuals— redistributing the influence to those who will be impacted by the decision.

## JOBS IN WHICH YOU CAN BE INVOLVED

There are many careers and volunteering opportunities that directly impact the communities we live in. Here are a few jobs in this sphere that play a massive part in the development, management, and creation of space in the world.

### GARDEN DESIGNERS OR LANDSCAPE ARCHITECTS

Garden designers and landscape architects outline a vision for a space. They design the hard landscaping, for example, paths and walls, as well as soft landscaping, such as planting, deciding layout, function, as well as which materials to use.

### STRUCTURAL ENGINEERS

This type of engineer designs structures so they are capable of withstanding use and environmental elements. You could work on a variety of different building projects and developments, including housing, shopping centers, museums, offices, bridges, or even offshore rigs and space satellites.

## INTERIOR DESIGNERS

Interior designers specialize in creating functional and aesthetically pleasing interior spaces. They work with clients to develop design concepts and plans that take into account factors such as spatial layout, lighting, color, and materials, as well as the unique style and personality of their clients.

## ENVIRONMENTAL ENGINEERS

Environmental engineers use the principles of engineering, soil science, biology, and chemistry to develop solutions to environmental problems. They work to improve recycling, waste disposal, and water and air pollution.

## ARCHITECTS

Architects develop plans and visual concepts for buildings and structures, considering engineering, functionality, safety, and aesthetics.

## VIDEO GAME DESIGNERS

To create a video game, designers imagine plots, characters, and visuals. The skills applied to creating very intricate virtual worlds, which interact and respond in many different ways, have begun to be introduced into the world of real-life architecture. Video game design technology has done nothing but advance and improve the world of architecture—enabling faster, more efficient, and more accurate 3D concepts. Many game designers are now being headhunted by architecture firms that see the opportunity and overlap within both branches of design.

## DID YOU KNOW?
—

Backup Ukraine is an ingenious example of how innovative technology can be used for positive outcomes. Backup Ukraine is a partnership between Virtue, Polycam, the Blue Shield Denmark, and the Danish UNESCO National Commission, and it sets out to create virtual assets of real-life places and items, such as monuments and buildings, in a bid to conserve Ukraine's cultural history. Volunteers and residents in Ukraine are encouraged to use the Backup Ukraine app to scan as much of their country as possible, so that even if destroyed there are 3D models that can be used for re-creation, acknowledgment, and remembrance.

# BOSCO VERTICALE,

# VERTICAL FOREST

BOERI STUDIO (S. BOERI, G. BARRECA,
G. LA VARRA), MILAN, ITALY

With limited space available in already overdeveloped and overcrowded cities, a forest in the sky could be the future of architecture, design, and landscaping. Such a project, known as Bosco Verticale ("Vertical Forest"), was opened in 2014, and comprises two densely residential buildings standing proud in urban Milan, where they are a showcase of what could be. They are buildings that have taken bold steps forward.

Now home to almost 20,000 trees, shrubs, and perennial plants, after a five-year build, the Bosco Verticale houses 300 non-plant residents in affordable homes in the heart of the Porta Nuova district of Milan. Not only does the biodiverse array of greenery provide a screen to noise and air pollution, but it also converts an average of 44,000 lb (20,000 kg) of carbon each year, and this is vital given the impacts of air toxicity on health and well-being.

# IT'S ONLY A MATTER OF TIME BEFORE PLANTS BECOME THE MAIN FEATURE IN ARCHITECTURE AND DESIGN

For me, such inner-city residential tower blocks represent the type of biological, biophilic, creative architecture that is much needed as we look for solutions. The best and most prevalent part of these buildings is their beauty—nature is stunning and does most of the design work. The many textures and colors of the plants soften the impact of the 11-story buildings, helping them blend into the blues and grays of the sky. What would usually be very linear and jagged buildings have become light and blurred pieces of art. It does make you wonder, why aren't all buildings forests in the sky?

Maybe it's time for us to hand parts of our overly designed cities back to nature as part of the search for balance, beauty, and benefit.

## WHAT CAN YOU DO?

For a moment, it's always good to close your eyes and try to rid yourself of all the limitations, constrictions, and conditions that you've accepted to be normal. What is normal? Imagine if you had the chance to create a space without the influence of tradition or what's already there. See where your imagination takes you—I always like to try and work backward from the most wild and radical ideas. Let others say "no" to your suggestions—we have to be bold when it comes to the future of space.

Encouraged by the outstanding example of the Bosco Verticale, you, too, can start to integrate nature into typically lifeless spaces. If you have access to a balcony, what's stopping you? Pots and planters, hanging baskets, climbers, and trailers are all ways you can blend nature into your everyday life.

It's only a matter of time before plants become the main feature in architecture and design. We are all designers in our own way, and we may not quite realize the impacts of small decisions we make based on our space—a plant on the windowsill might bring joy to an overlooking neighbor or a passerby. Design needs to bring people and plants together, and we can all play a part in encouraging that level of connection.

# GREENING THE GRAY

There are many ways in which you can bring planting to your surroundings. In densely populated, inner-city spaces, there are often opportunities for gardens on balconies and rooftops. The modern garden is all about using floor space, vertical space, or planters creatively. Small, urban spaces drive the need for multifunctional plants—those that hold purpose and benefit for a plethora of reasons.

## PLANT YOUR OWN POLLUTION BARRIER

Whether we like it or not, sound, light, and air pollution are major issues both for the climate and our health. With air toxicity, for example, at an all-time high, especially in towns and cities, it's important that we seek solutions to reduce the damage caused by pollution. In London alone, where I live, there is an excess of 4,100 premature deaths each year due to the impacts of air pollution. But how can we help both planet and people to combat it?

One thing we all can do at home, in the office, or on the street is to incorporate more plants to combat air, noise, and sight pollution. Here's what I've done to bring plants into a space to address air and sound pollution while also creating a beautiful, intimate space to enjoy. You, too, could achieve this by planting a pollution barrier either in a bed or up on a balcony in a pot.

## CLIMBERS FOR COVER

It often shocks me just how unexplored, in design, the use of climbers is. Drainpipes, brick walls, and metal fences are just waiting to be prettified with often-scented floral vines that can bring a place to life. There are climbers for any surface and any canvas—I like to view them as plant graffiti, with colors and textures that introduce layers of interest to an otherwise bland

### POLLUTION BARRIER IDEAS
—

- cherry laurel (*Prunus laurocerasus*): wildlife friendly, noise reducing, pollution combating;
- elaeagnus (*Elaeagnus*): wildlife friendly, pollution combating, has edible berries;
- hawthorn (*Crataegus monogyna*): wildlife friendly, has edible berries, slows water run-off;
- red robin (*Photinia × fraseri* 'Red Robin'): wildlife friendly, noise reducing;
- tawhiwhi (*Pittosporum*): wildlife friendly, pollution combating, has fragrant flowers.

space. Evergreen varieties are a good choice if you want to have a green screen for privacy or hide an eyesore. On the next page, you'll find Your Guide to Climbers to help you pick.

Because climbers often need something to climb up, you could repurpose pretty much any material—wire, rope, or old trellising—to support them. However, climbers can be stronger than you expect, so before planting always consider pipes, poles, and surfaces, such as a brick wall, that might be impacted by the climber. To guide it up the surface, tie it in loosely but securely at regular intervals, using figure-eight knots. Never tie the stems so tightly that they are damaged as the plant grows; also avoid using sharp/rigid tying materials.

If you don't have a suitable support structure, opt for a climber that will cling onto walls, drainpipes, and most other surfaces—something like a climbing hydrangea (*Hydrangea barbara*). Some climbers such as ivy (*Hedera*) are self-supporting, but they may leave marks on the surface to which they are clinging.

You can plant your climber directly into suitable soil in the ground or in a pot. Choose the size of pot based on how big you'd like your climber to grow. When growing any plant, especially on a balcony or a rooftop, check that the combined weight of the plant and container doesn't compromise any structures they might stand on.

# CLIMBERS

Climbers are, by far, one of the most efficient and creative plants that can sometimes spread far over buildings, structures, and even mature trees. Their considerable qualities do make you wonder why they're not mandatory on all vertical structures. They offer so many options to bring color, wildlife, and edible food to otherwise bland and boring vertical spaces—plus they're not hard to grow.

### PASSION FLOWER (*PASSIFLORA*)

This quirky and intricate vine bears the well-known, tropical passion fruits—but beware, some species have more appetizing fruits than others. The flowers alone would be a unique addition to your garden, with their funky colors and shapes in summer and fall.

### SWEET PEA (*LATHYRUS ODORATUS*)

Although an annual climber, sweet pea is worth putting in the time and effort to plant every year. While the flowers and pods aren't edible, the blooms make fragrant and vibrant bunches that you can put in vases to lift any room in your house.

### BOUGAINVILLEA (*BOUGAINVILLEA*)

This climber takes my mind straight to subtropical climates, where sun and sea are close. It's often hot pink, deep purple, or bright orange. Summer blooms may start to become more of a feature in previously colder climates, such as the UK, as temperatures start to rise.

### CLEMATIS (*CLEMATIS*)

This beautiful flowering climber will brighten up any space, year-round. Some clematis also have additional uses: for example, the leaves and seeds of *C. ligusticifolia* were once eaten as a black pepper substitute when black pepper was very rare and expensive.

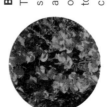

## TRUMPET VINE (*CAMPSIS RADICANS*)

With its unique, often peachy orange color, the trumpet vine plays jazz to those passing by with its graceful, muted, pulled-back, instrument-like flowers from late summer. Trumpets that attract pollinators? Surely onto a winner here. Butterflies, hummingbirds, and bees all join in this symphony of nature.

## CLIMBING HYDRANGEA (*HYDRANGEA BARBARA*)

A plant that does well in partial shade is always useful in built-up, dense areas, where light levels can often be low because of the multitude of buildings. It flowers in summer.

## VINE (*VITIS*)

The number of things you can do with grapes will blow your mind: from using the fruit to refresh and replenish (frozen grapes on a hot day are a personal favorite); to the Arabic and Mediterranean dishes that include grape leaves. Of course, you can also make wine with the fruit.

## HONEYSUCKLE (*LONICERA*)

This climber, which attracts many pollinators, is great for planting against a trellis, a fence, or a lightweight structure because it clings only lightly. You could also grow it up a drainpipe. Depending on the species, it can flower at any time of year.

## WISTERIA (*WISTERIA*)

You know when you've walked past wisteria—you are instantly pulled in by the perfumed scent from its cascading flowers. While growing up in Notting Hill, some of my dream houses were bedecked in wisteria in late spring, when it starts to bloom.

## JASMINE (*JASMINUM OFFICINALE*)

You'll know when you pass this iconic plant because you'll be immediately drawn to its scent in summer. This is often extracted as an oil to be used in perfumes, and it epitomizes the floral notes that are now added to many beauty products.

# BROOKLYN

# GRANGE

BEN FLANNER AND ANASTASIA COLE PLAKIAS
NEW YORK CITY

There's no denying that there's a universal idea of what a farm is. It's ingrained in nursery rhymes, in tales, and is still very much a reality today. It is acres of land with fences, grazing cows, and monocultural fields of crops. How do we reimagine a very bound idea of what a farm is, what it looks like, and how it functions?

The gray and gridded, high-rise design of New York City really is a statement of modernity. The hustle and bustle of The Big Apple is the least likely place you would expect to stumble across a farm, yet in that city a movement is emerging that is actively redefining what a farm could be. Who knew you could grow radishes on rooftops?

Brooklyn Grange exists as a trio of rooftop farms, 5.6 acres (2.26 hectares) in total, growing organic food as well as producing local honey;

all three of them are based on a community-supported model. Starting off in Long Island City with the first farm in 2010, Brooklyn Grange Farm expanded to take over the Brooklyn Navy Yard in 2012, and Liberty View in Sunset Park in 2019. The three farms now produce an impressive 100,000lb (45,000kg) of organic fruits and vegetables annually.

With such high yields, you'd expect a cutthroat approach to operations and the business model to achieve such big numbers—yet Brooklyn Grange Farm certainly does have charm. With a strong community-led ethos, their farms have become a crucial part of the local society being a free source of fresh produce for low-income New Yorkers; classrooms for visiting schools; beautiful spaces for musicians, events, and programs; an area providing employment as well as career

opportunities that weren't otherwise available; and, at the very least, they are an escape in the clouds from the rat race going on down below. Thus, Brooklyn Grange Farm is a farm in name yet is so much more in nature.

Its multifaceted, rooftop approach encourages opportunities to spark interest in a wide range of people. With a menu of different ways into the farm, there is choice of how anyone can engage with the space. Brooklyn Grange offers a friendlier, more welcoming feel to a traditional farm, which typically is an area with "keep out" signs. It also begs the question "why can't farms be more friendly, multifunctional, and conscious both socially and environmentally?"

## WHAT CAN YOU DO?

Wouldn't it be amazing if our way of navigating cities were purely through gardens and parks rather than roads and streets? Brooklyn Grange Farm in New York, to me, is a good example of thinking with as few boundaries and as much ambition as possible. Such a complete change in perceptions is what urban growing requires. With space at a premium, asking the question "Why can't I grow here?" has never been more relevant

and well received, whether it's through structured organizations such as Brooklyn Grange Farm or maybe employee pressure in an office that has an accessible balcony or rooftop. Any space (especially outdoors) deserves to be green and full of life.

Yes, that sounds great and super-simple on paper; so why aren't all cities filled with plants spilling off buildings, and trees populating all our streets? You need to demand a change of policy to one that requires more green urban infrastructure in developments, old and new, and also, more importantly (and excitingly), you can get experimenting to start your very own small space revolution. Of course, it's a bit of a challenge— but isn't everything?

Urban spaces often imply small, shallow, or awkward sites but who says they can't attract bees or grow berries. I would start to think about how, if possible, you can optimize the growing conditions. Increasing depth for root growth can help but isn't essential—different plants can adapt and even thrive in improbable sites. A pot or a planter is a great place to start before you go full- blown and emulate Brooklyn Grange Farm. Your actions might just trigger someone else's imagination and encourage them to join you in re-greening somewhere. You can grow anywhere—it's time to redefine what or where a garden can be.

# WITH A STRONG COMMUNITY-LED ETHOS, THEIR FARMS HAVE BECOME A CRUCIAL PART OF THE LOCAL SOCIETY

# GROW EDIBLES
# VERTICALLY

The satisfaction of growing your own food is not to be overlooked or underestimated. Taking your health and where you source your food into your own hands is empowering, to say the least. When you think about growing food you immediately assume you need many acres of farmland ... But what if you didn't require all that space. What would seem like an obvious yet surprisingly unexplored feature in almost every space is the vertical one, which has become evident as we've developed, urbanized, and built up (see p.078). It seems very contradictory to use the word "developed" because we've disturbed and destroyed ecosystems to create highly dense living spaces— with no regard to working with the local ecology or nature. It doesn't seem very developed to me!

There are opportunities everywhere. Have you ever thought about what you could do with any vertical space on or around, for example, a shop, a school, or any other building? Who knew that a wall that is typically there to divide, separate, and provide a harsh boundary could be so welcoming and inviting? Being an almost untouched canvas in the gardening world, it doesn't take much to make use of a wall to beautify, attract wildlife, and bring food to your plate. It would also create more opportunities for people to coexist—both with each other and with nature.

One thing I've realized is that you can't wait for change— you have to try and inspire it. Here are some ideas, both aspirational and practical, that will help create those much-needed food oases.

You can sow plants from seed—start off in modules indoors—or buy plug plants. See also Creating Sowing Modules, p.128. Water regularly, especially when the plants are young, and remove any weeds promptly.

## PLANTING IDEAS FOR VERTICAL VEGETABLE GROWING
—

Here, I am growing
(*top row*):
- sage (*Salvia*),
- rosemary (*Salvia rosmarinus*);
  (*second row*):
- parsley (*Petroselinum*),
- strawberries (*Fragaria*);
  (*third row*):
- sorrel (*Rumex sanguineus*),
- salad greens;
  (*bottom row*):
- mint (*Mentha*).

⊙ Shallow-rooted salad greens and herbs are perfect for growing in small containers, such as this ladder, for produce all year round.

## FOOD ON A LADDER

This cost-effective leaning ladder is a great option if you're in need of greenery and vegetables yet don't have much space. One advantage is that you don't need to drill into a wall to have the living wall of your dreams—simply lean the food ladder up against a wall (see p.091). If building the ladder shown is a bit daunting for your DIY skills, a simpler alternative might be to repurpose an ordinary ladder on which to sit or hang pots.

If building one yourself, you can use upcycled and reclaimed timber, and it can be as long or as wide as you like, to suit your gardening needs. Use liners to protect the wood inside the planters from rotting, and paint on a sealant to preserve and enhance the timber.

## UPCYCLED WOODEN PALLETS

Another way you might be able to create a vertical vegetable feature would be to reuse wooden pallets. These rigid and already stable structures offer the perfect home for plants without having to do too much prep work. Pallets also allow for the option to be flexible with space and size. A small space might cater to only one pallet, while if more width, height, and depth are available you could have multiple pallets. To create more floor space, the pallet or pallets could lean up against a wall, or be drilled into the wall using anchors and screws, providing a whole host of combinations and options to fit the space you're looking to green up.

Pallets come in different shapes and sizes, often giving character and interest, but you can always adapt them by sanding them down and adding a lick of paint if you want to create a more refreshed and vibrant vibe in your space. See p.126 for more detailed instructions on how to upcycle a wooden pallet that is suitable for planting.

More than a million UK and 19 million US residents live in "food deserts." This means an area that has limited access to affordable and nutritious food. In contrast, an area with greater access to supermarkets and stores with fresh foods may be called a "food oasis."

## LIVING VEGETABLE WALL

Who said you can't integrate food growing with ornamental plants? While a living wall is aspirational for many, there's no arguing that one like this creates an immersive space. By using an existing wall as the solid structure to build on, this is an all-in approach to create a long-term, flourishing canvas of wilderness, but it does require specialized expertise to ensure structural integrity and irrigation. As such, this is very much what you should be aiming for when it comes to inner-city spaces (or any space for that matter!).

While installing a living wall may not be particularly cheap, as the technology advances the hope is that it will become the new normal. One thing's for sure—living vegetable walls are a significant improvement on the brutal materials of brick walls or metal structures, both aesthetically and environmentally.

One pocket planter might not make much impact but when you've got many together they really do become a piece of art. Many pocket planters already come with drainage and irrigation infrastructure to ensure the plants are healthy and thrive, even in limited space.

# GROWING YOUR OWN FOOD

**KEY**

—

○ SOW
○ PLANT
○ HARVEST

| | JAN | FEB | MAR | APR | MAY | JUN | JUL | AUG | SEPT | OCT | NOV | DEC |
|---|---|---|---|---|---|---|---|---|---|---|---|---|

**BEETS**
*Beta vulgaris subsp. vulgaris*

**CHARD**
*Beta vulgaris subsp. cicla var. flavescens*

**LETTUCE**
*Lactuca*

**MINT**
*Mentha*

**NASTURTIUM**
*Tropaeolum majus*

**PARSLEY**
*Petroselinum crispum*

**RADISH**
*Raphanus sativus*

**ROSEMARY**
*Salvia rosmarinus, syn.*
*Rosmarinus officinalis*

**SAGE**
*Salvia officinalis*

**SORREL**
*Rumex acetosa*

**STRAWBERRIES**
*Fragaria × ananassa*
*and F. vesca*

**SPINACH**
*Spinacia oleracea*

**THYME**
*Thymus*

# REWILD

/ˌriːˈwaɪld/

**Rewild**
*verb*
to protect an enviroment and
return it to its natural state

# WILDLIFE

## IS OFTEN THE FIRST THING TO BE DISMISSED WHEN

# COMPROMISE IS NEEDED

There's something freeing about being in a wilderness, often conjured by childlike memories. In such a wonderland, distraction after distraction takes you on an unexpected adventure: some slight movement over here; a flash of color over there; what was that unusual noise? Through curiosity and awe, nature occupies the mind in the most wonderful way. If we accept that nature benefits our mental health—what does a lack of nature do?

The importance of wildlife and plants really does all start to make sense when you think hard about it. Science allows us to try and measure change but there's only so much science can tell us—just imagine what we don't know. The soundscape, for example, has changed dramatically over the last 50 years—with cars and planes frequently dominating even the most remote places. Do we even think about how this affects wildlife?

While growing up, many of us were taught to have a phobia of insects, spiders, and other creepy crawlies. Although this might seem just a small issue, such lessons are amplified on a grander societal scale in the way that wildlife is often the first thing to be dismissed when compromise is needed. Can you imagine that in built-up spaces, where we've displaced most wildlife—where it struggles to thrive and even exist—that we're scared of it?

Very complex ecosystems and habitats for wildlife and plants are diminishing on our watch, but it doesn't need to be that way. By default, nature has no choice in the matter. However, it's now time we give wildlife and plants a bigger voice. Although there is no one perfect answer, we must constantly try to understand the consequential imbalances of the human population to ensure that we respect the unwritten laws of coexistence.

## In conversation with
## TOM MASSEY

I first met Tom—a garden designer—on set while filming *Your Garden Made Perfect* for the BBC. It was through our shared belief that nature enhances landscapes, communities, and well-being that our friendship bloomed.

**TAYSHAN: So here we are, in your Resilient Garden display at RHS Hampton Court Palace Garden Festival 2023. What intrigues me is what does rewilding mean to you?**

**TOM:** For me, rewilding is a term that means a lot of things to a lot of different people. So there's the technical rewilding term, which involves the reintroduction of species that have gone extinct [in the wild or in a particular area], or letting things just return to nature. However, my Resilient Garden is much more about a wilder aesthetic, and it includes a mix of plants that coexist in a more ecological fashion. So there's the mix of perennials, grasses, some herbs, and trees—all intermingled and planted in this kind of matrix-like display. To me, that evokes a wild feeling, even though it's not a wild space.

**TAYSHAN: Your garden's almost bringing together those layers that were often seen as separate things: for example, you may get a garden of perennials or a garden with grasses and fruit or vegetables. But here, it's a big mix.**

**TOM:** Yes, my Resilient Garden is certainly intermingled. This concept of planting is called the "forest" garden, and it essentially mimics the layers of a natural forest. So you've got the tree layer, the canopy layer, then bigger shrubs, and then ground cover like the wild strawberries and creeping plants that will cover the soil. They are providing food for humans, like the strawberries. You can also eat the day lilies and, obviously, the pears off the pear tree. This forest garden also has food for pollinators and shelter for insects. And you're creating a space that functions both for humans and the wildlife that we share the planet with.

**TAYSHAN:** That's equally as important.

**TOM:** Yeah, equally, if not more important.

**TAYSHAN:** And so, how much do you integrate rewilding into your design, philosophy, and ideology?

**TOM:** I try to incorporate a wild feel in my designs or be inspired by the surrounding landscape. I think there's a lot of debate around rewilding, and whether gardens should be wild. Or should gardens be gardens? For me, I think there is not really a distinction. You know, our gardens are natural spaces where we have an opportunity to create a deep connection to nature. And I think the more wild they feel, the more I feel immersed and comfortable and at home in them.

**TAYSHAN:** And what would you say to those that may not be so on board with the rewilding kind of way?

**TOM:** I think we must move on from seeing our gardens as these pristine, sprayed, clipped, formal spaces that we're forcing nature out of. We need to view our gardens as the spaces that we share with nature and that are part of a much wider ecosystem. Gardens in the UK alone equate to something like the size of Wales. And if everyone made changes to the way that they garden by introducing a bit more wildness to their spaces, we'd have a huge tranche of rewilded landscape in this country. So, to make big change, I think gardeners have to come together and not fight each other.

**TAYSHAN:** And how did you come to this way of thinking? Was it always part of your garden design philosophy, or did it evolve?

**TOM:** It was through my mum, who always made us go on long walks in the countryside. We spent a lot of time in Cornwall, and we were set free to explore the cliffs and roam the landscape. So I think, from a very early age, for me, that connection to nature was really important and made me feel at home and comfortable. You know, mental health is a big part of it as well. I think I'm inspired much more by wild landscapes than I am by formal gardens, so I try and bring that into my designs.

# THE
# HIGH

# LINE

NEW YORK CITY

The High Line is a rewilding project like no other. Once destined for demolition, a derelict train line that had previously been a vital transportation link cutting through New York City is now a hot spot for plants, people, and pollinators. A campaign led by the local community all started when the first questions were asked in 1983, such as: "What to do with this unused space?"

Those questions helped ideas evolve, and momentum grew. By 1999, the High Line became a topic of wide debate. On the one hand, Mayor Rudy Giuliani signed a demolition order while, on the other hand, there was acknowledgment of a budding and abundant ecosystem flourishing on the unused railroad tracks.

Without any certainty or assurances as to what might become of the High Line, the Friends of the High Line launched an ideas competition. The response they received was overwhelming: 720 entries from 36 different countries came flooding in, and the High Line was well and truly back on the action map.

Between 2004 and 2006, with support from the current New York City mayor, Michael Bloomberg, a team of experts was assembled to plan and cocreate an artistic, multipurpose, accessible space in the urban canopy. One of those experts was the world-renowned garden designer Piet Oudolf.

Piet's admiration for the architectural qualities of any plant shines through his work and is exemplified by the matrix of grasses and perennial flowers now weaving through New York's old railroad line. His unconventional planting style means that there is year-round consideration for the environment, with seed heads, leaves, and flowers left standing, even in their wilted, decomposing state. Subsequently, this vegetation provides food, shelter, and protection for wildlife over the coldest winter months.

## CELEBRATING INSECTS ON THE HIGH LINE

Central to the railroad line's transformation was
the provision of a symbiotic relationship between
flowering plants and pollinating insects as well as
the greater web of life, including humans. In order
to achieve this, the planners selected specific
plants, including native ones, to attract particular
insects. They also preserved and created
appropriate habitats such as bee hotels and
water features. For examples of which insects
have been spotted on which plants see the
biodiversity table (opposite).

## WHAT CAN YOU DO?

The transformation of the High Line in New York
City leaves me feeling inspired and is a reminder
to always dream big. The persistence of the local
community in pushing to retain, protect, and
enhance the already prevalent rewilding of the
railroad line sets the bar high when it comes to
community activism. It gets me thinking about
what could be achieved in my own local
community. Could we see the Ladbroke Grove
High Line come to life at some point in the near
future, to replace the Westway, which was built in
the mid 1960s as part of major investment in the
A40(M)? Since then, the number of cars driving
along Westway over my community has reached
over 100,000 a day. If ever there was a case for a
High Line–inspired project in London, this is it.

Other takeaways from the planting on the High
Line are that its perennial planting programs serve
wildlife year-round and that seed heads are left on
the plants to reseed naturally or to be harvested
for sowing elsewhere. Why don't you see which
insects land on which plants you grow?

| High Line plant | Related pollinator/insect |
| --- | --- |
| American chokecherry (*Prunus virginiana*) | Lunate zale moth (*Zale lunata*) |
| Large-leaved cucumber tree (*Magnolia macrophylla*) | Tumbling flower beetle (*Mordellidae* family) |
| Blue giant hyssop (*Agastache foeniculum*) | Great spangled fritillary butterfly (*Speyeria cybele*) |
| Bluebird smooth aster (*Symphyotrichum laeve* 'Bluebird') | Syrphid fly adult and larva (*Sphaerophoria philanthus*) |
| Bur oak (*Quercus macrocarpa*) | Edwards' hairstreak caterpillar (*Satyrium edwardsii*) |
| Butterfly weed (*Asclepias tuberosa*) | Large milkweed bug (*Oncopeltus fasciatus*) |
| Claire Grace bergamot (*Monarda* 'Claire Grace') | Eastern carpenter bee (*Xylocopa virginica*) |
| Grow-low fragrant sumac (*Rhus aromatica* 'Gro-Low') | Bristle-legged moth (*Schreckensteinia erythriella*) |
| New Jersey tea (*Ceanothus americanus*) | Bumblebee (*Bombus genus*); and poor miner bee (*Pseudopanurgus pauper*) |
| Purple coneflower (*Echinacea purpurea*) | Any cavity-nesting bee |
| Sassafras (*Sassafras albidum*) | Promethea silk moth (*Callosamia promethea*) and Spicebush swallowtail (*Papilio troilus*) |
| Short-toothed mountain mint (*Pycnanthemum muticum*) | European honey bee (*Apis mellifera*) |
| Showy goldenrod (*Solidago speciosa*) | Wavy-lined emerald geometer moth caterpillar (*Synchlora aerata*) |
| Buttonbush (*Cephalanthus occidentalis*) | Hydrangea sphinx moth (*Darapsa versicolor*) ; and Titan sphinx moth (*Aellopos titan*) |
| Summer sweet (*Clethra alnifolia*) | Organ pipe mud dauber wasp (*Trypoxylon politum*) |
| Swamp azalea (*Rhododendron viscosum*) | Azalea miner bee (*Andrena cornelli*) |

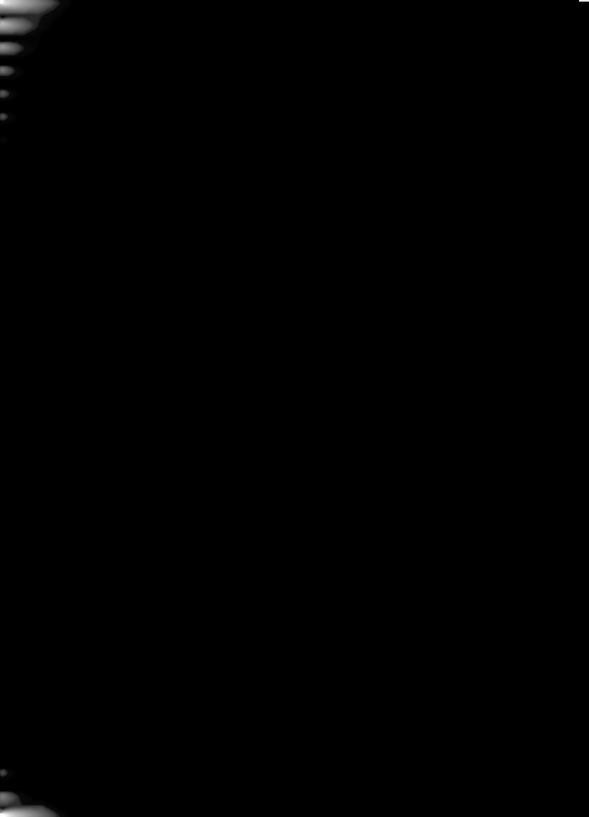

## YOU WILL NEED

—

o Repurposed tin cans, thoroughly washed
o Combi drill driver with a hammer function
o ¼-in (7-mm) drill bit, suitable for masonry
o Plastic-coated garden wire
o Reclaimed glass bottle rack, not too heavy! Ours is 3×3 and made from timber
o Wall anchors such as hooks with screw ends—the number will depend on the size of your bottle rack
o Pencil for marking wall
o Spirit level
o Wall plugs to fit ¼-in (7mm) holes
o Hammer
o Multipurpose, peat-free potting mix

### Pollinator-friendly plants

o Angelonia (*Angelonia*)
o Bellflower (*Campanula*)
o Ivy (*Hedera*)

**01**

On each tin can, drill two small holes just below the rim, ½ in (1cm) apart and large enough for the garden wire to thread through (see step 2). This place will now be the back edge of the can and is where it will be fitted to the bottle rack. On the bottom of the tin can, drill a few holes, ½ in (1cm) apart, on the front edge, to allow drainage.

**02**

Loop the garden wire through the holes below the rim in each tin can, and fasten each one to the bottle rack wherever you'd like to place them.

**03**

Using a pencil, mark the wall where you would like to place the first hook, and then, aided by a spirit level, mark the second hole position. Use the hammer setting on the drill to make a hole in the brick wall; this should be deep enough for the wall plug. Then tap in a wall plug using the hammer. Screw a hook into the wall plug, by hand, until its hook is upright. Then drill and insert a second hook, in the same way.

**04**

Position your rack directly onto the hooks (as here), or use garden wire to secure the rack to the hooks. Plant up your tins or fill them with bamboo cut to size for a bug hotel.

# CONTAINER POND

## YOU WILL NEED
—

- Watertight planter or container
- Various sizes of gravel, rocks, stones, bricks, or logs
- Rainwater
- Aquatic plants

**Aquatic plants for a container**
- Common water starwort (*Callitriche stagnalis*)
- Flowering rush (*Butomus umbellatus*)
- Lesser spearwort (*Ranunculus flammula*)
- Miniature water lily (*Nymphaea* 'Pygmaea Helvola')

An often overlooked, yet simple, opportunity to bring a whole new layer of biodiversity to your garden or green space can be achieved by having a pond in a container. Aquatic plants can thrive in a pond, purifying the water and helping to create the perfect spot to extend the micro-ecosystem in your garden or green space. Not only will such a pond offer new opportunities for food and water for wildlife, but it might also provide a home or breeding ground.

As well as having wildlife benefits, a container pond in your garden is a wonderful spot where you can pause, absorb, and relax. Water has a peaceful and soothing way of calming the mind—being reflective and mesmerizing in appearance. A forever changing picture is revealed as your eyes adjust to the water, and what's below its surface becomes clearer—a whole David Attenborough documentary's worth of wildlife activity comes into view. Looking into a pond is always fun—for young and old alike. If that alone isn't worth introducing a container pond, I don't know what is!

**01**

Ensure your container is stable and firmly positioned on the ground. Then place a mixture of gravel, rocks, stones, and logs in it, to create different heights for the variety of wildlife that might seek shelter or a home in your pond. Install a mini ramp to help any wildlife enter and exit your pond.

**02**

Position the plants in your pond, and imagine the water level—make sure plant soil will be covered and foliage will sit above the water line. You can use smaller gravel/stones to secure the plants in place.

**03**

Fill your container pond with collected rainwater. Avoid tap water if possible because it contains chemicals that aren't as wildlife friendly as rainwater. Then sit back and enjoy watching the wildlife go crazy as your pond evolves.

**SUNKEN POND**

If you have the space, why not position your pond container in the ground? For this, you need to dig a hole that is the size of your chosen container.

/ˌriːˈpɜː.pəs/

# REPURPOSE

**Repurpose**
verb
To find or adapt for a new use
or purpose

# WE REALLY NEED TO NORMALIZE REUSING, RECYCLING, AND REPURPOSING

We've extracted an inordinate amount of natural resources from the planet, creating a nonstop, ever-increasing conveyor belt of newness. We've developed this culture of there never being enough—always wanting more and more. And viewing everything as objects with a transactional value is so dangerous and takes away so much—the stories, the meaning, the feeling. Objects can shortcut long-term purpose for short-term satisfaction. There are so many reasons we should give a second lease on life to already existing items—whether that's in construction, fashion, or food. We really need to normalize reusing, recycling, and repurposing. Such actions should not be looked down upon or trivialized. There are so many benefits, and it's always important to consider where something is coming from and what it could become.

The joy of giving new life to old clothes, for example, is an act of storytelling, extending the legacy of what would otherwise be just a piece of material. Imagine the people who once wore the clothing—where to, and why. The places it saw, the conversations it heard, the people it met. All of a sudden, trying to find the right size, the right fit, or a style that suits you is an adventure. First impressions are always important, but they're not everything—get a feel, an understanding, and a deeper appreciation for the article. Think about who made the clothing, for better or for worse. How many hours of craft went into producing that item? Were the people responsible for it exploited in any way? Sadly, it's possible that an element of sacrifice is involved during the creation of any piece of clothing—some cases are more extreme than others.

# I'VE ALWAYS MADE A CONSCIOUS EFFORT TO REUSE MATERIALS

Fortunately, there are hidden gems out there—one-of-a-kind treasures—that are waiting on the racks of secondhand stores for you. There's always a sense of self-discovery when it comes to thrift shopping—your options aren't limited to what the stores think you might want to buy. It's a bit more of a lottery. Don't get me wrong; there is some outrageous stuff in secondhand stores, but that's all part of the fun. Throwing a sequined, oversize jacket from the '70s on the shoulders of a friend never gets old.

It's not just clothes that carry those legacy tales into the present day. I get more out of acknowledging the resistant and resilient stories that certain materials have to tell. In projects, I've always made a conscious effort to reuse materials in any space, leaning on their characters to create interest and intrigue. The rich history of worn and torn metals, stone, glass—whatever you can get your hands on—tells a story about each item and its surroundings. It has a new purpose, a renewed destiny.

The use of repurposed materials was central to the design for the Hands Off Mangrove garden at RHS Chelsea Flower Show (see p.014). On such a big platform, it was important that we showcased many ways in which materials could be repurposed, but equally we needed to lean into the stories that those materials might tell or provoke thought and feeling.

The main sculpture in the show garden, standing at 14½ ft (4.5 m) tall, comprised upcycled reinforced bars of Corten Steel bolted together. The choice of such weathered, rough, and raw material was made to encourage a sense of just how up against it we are both socially and environmentally. The upcycled, mixed, crushed-concrete path related to urban development during the 1960s, when the pillars of the Westway, in the London Royal Borough of Kensington & Chelsea, were first being constructed. With their exposed, contrasting colors and textures, upcycled, rusty, corrugated-iron panels mentally transported the Flower Show visitors to the

Caribbean, while old cooking pots were used to grow food such as tomatoes, strawberries, and even lettuce.

There are ways—as a business or at home—that you, too, can repurpose materials, thus reducing your waste and also improving your resource efficiency; this makes complete sense financially. Being aware of your waste means you think twice before purchasing unnecessary items and before continuing to hoard no-longer-used items.

Why not declutter your space and declutter your mind? Really think about what function everything has. Does it add to the design of your space? Does it occupy a mental and/or sentimental place?

When you realize that pretty much everything once began life in the ground, as a natural material, you'll become more conscious of its history—the good, the bad, and the ugly. We can't change or undo what has been done, but we do have the power to influence the present and the future. We have to consider what we choose to evolve, to preserve, and to conserve.

Humans have created wonderful, amazing, life-changing technologies and inventions, which impact and influence our everyday lives, but equally humans have a long and continuous history, often suppressed, of abuse and exploitation. It's important we seek ways of creating, without ripping off or ill-treating the planet and people—that, for me, is true innovation and entrepreneurship.

# THE ONION GARDEN

JENS JAKOBSEN
LONDON, UK

It was a cold winter's day and the Grow to Know team was on its way to visit a neglected rooftop garden in the heart of London Victoria. A nature-enthused teacher at Westminster City School had reached out to Grow to Know in the hope that they could turn the currently underused, urban rooftop into a sanctuary garden for plants and people.

It's always so energizing meeting teachers who are passionate about creating connections to nature. As our cheerful chat came to a close, our client, who was a Welsh biology teacher, insisted we follow him on a short, five-minute wander. He didn't really tell us where we were going or what we were going to see—he just said that the scene would take our breath away.

The walk cut through some of the most corporate cityscapes in London, with the glass windows seemingly cleaned on a daily basis—not a speck of dust or a smudge in sight. I really do feel small at times in London. After turning a few corners, we came across a sign that read, "We all laugh in the same language." My shoulders relaxed and I took a deep breath, as we heard joy

## THE PURPOSE OF THE ONION GARDEN WAS TO SHOW HOW NATURE HAS EVERYTHING WE NEED TO INSPIRE, LEARN, AND BE AWED BY

coming from behind some wilderness that I was trying to make sense of—I didn't quite know where to look! I was like a kid in a candy store, fascinated by all the quirky and architectural artwork dotted around the garden.

I turned to my colleague in astonishment. "Are those ... are those dead leaf stacks?!" Every step revealed a new discovery. "Look! Is that a cinnamon tree?! Cinnamon doesn't grow on trees like that—does it?!"

The garden pulled us in many different directions at the same time. If you know me, you'd understand that it completely matched my energy (I'm known for being distracted and pulled in many directions at once).

"Hello!" we heard from behind a few bird-nest planters. "Bird-nest planters?" I hear you say. The planters we spotted were made from twigs in the style of a bird's nest, and held the soil in which seeds and plants could flourish.

"Welcome to The Onion Garden!" said a man who approached us with a warm smile and outstretched arms. Jens Jakobsen was his

name. He went on to explain that the purpose of The Onion Garden was to show how nature has everything we need to inspire, learn, and be awed by.

Jens saw something symbolic about the onion, full of life and full of vitamins. This was a fascination from deep in his childhood. To Jens, an onion is a ball of energy, ready to sprout into life. It represents the circle of life, ring by ring by ring. Jens looked to Ancient Egyptian practices to understand just how magical the onion is, because festivals and ceremonies would pivot around the onion—the Egyptians saw it as a way of appeasing the gods of the afterlife.

And there we were, in 2022, standing at the foot of an onion tree—an artistic expression on the importance of the onion. Its dead branches and twigs were constructed in a treelike fashion with onions hanging from them like baubles.
In a location so sterile, monocultural, and lacking in historical awareness, The Onion Garden is extremely rich in many ways: from the symbolism, to the purpose, to just how exposed it is. Open all

day and all night, Jens puts trust in the community to look after and respect the space. Isn't this just what we should all be aiming for? Whether it's an onion or a tulip, it's nature that gives us that commonality and that connection. Spaces like The Onion Garden just go to show the beauty and creativity that nature inspires—and are a massive credit to pioneers like Jens.

## WHAT CAN YOU DO?

When speaking with Jens, I always seem to have endless questions on how to do this, or what is that—it's like walking into a new world. Jens is truly a master crafter of natural materials, and therefore doesn't allow any of them to go to waste.

Why not think about what you might be able to do with fallen leaves, twigs, and even feathers? It's an artistic process that allows for full creativity and freedom. There's no right or wrong in this space. Who says an onion tree made from fallen twigs and bundles of onions can't be the focal point in a garden—not me!

# REUSING MATERIALS

Over many decades, we've accelerated the production of various industrial and everyday single-use materials, and we need to seize every opportunity to reuse them rather than view them as waste.

The things you can do with materials of any kind are limitless. Here are just a few ideas that might inspire you to come up with yet more ingenious solutions.

### CINDER BLOCKS

A building material often hidden from sight yet so crucial to the foundations of buildings we see daily is a cinder block. It can be used to build planters, by piling and spacing out several—not much else is needed but their weight to create a secure area in which to grow. How about planting in the cute pockets in the cinder blocks themselves. As you add soil and seeds within the gaps, make an abstract cinder block staircase of flowers with differing heights.

### GLASS BOTTLES

Because they come in all different shapes, sizes, and colors, glass bottles offer up a quite artistic yet resilient opportunity to get growing. Use them on your windowsill to plant something or to hold a small bouquet of flowers to brighten your day. Introduce solar-powered string lights to give your garden or balcony a magic feel. Choose glass bottles when watering plants or storing objects. Get technical and fashion up your own self-watering glass bottle—you might need some expert help for this.

### METALS

Repurposed metal has a massive part to play in our green spaces—there just needs to be a change of approach to the way metal can be used in gardening. For example, as a cheaper alternative to sourcing new items, why not transform small tin cans into planters to put on your kitchen table and windowsills. You could even lie a drawer-less filing cabinet on its back and fill it with soil and plants. Steel reinforcing mesh would make good trellis for climbers, while a metal welder could create something more intricate and bespoke with an old steel rod or rebar.

## PACKAGING

Whenever cardboard boxes are delivered to your home, always flatten, cut, or shred the box to continue the life cycle. Cardboard once came from trees rooted in the earth, so why not recycle it to support the growth of more trees? It is great in a compost heap, as a mulch, and as a weed suppressant when spread over the ground. Meanwhile, cardboard toilet paper rolls can become temporary planters to give seeds and seedlings a different home in which to develop (see p.128).

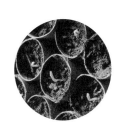

## PLASTIC BOTTLES

Plastics are everywhere in our daily lives, and the least we can do is make sure we reuse them as much as possible. However, this can be tricky to do. At the very minimum we've got to ensure that plastics aren't single use. Why not collect plastic bottles, cut them, string them up, and put holes in them to create hanging baskets or a makeshift watering can. Use them as slow-watering systems in your garden or cover your plants with them for protection. If you gather enough, you might even be able to create a greenhouse with them (see p.122).

## RAILROAD TIES

From planters to pergolas, railroad ties offer a naturalistic, flexible solution to any garden space—no matter the size. They can readily be cut, shaped, and secured, and so are an easy win for any garden. Use them as shallow retaining edges for your borders or pile them high to create a raised bed. Lie them flat to form a path so you can navigate conveniently between different spaces. Throw a couple of railroad ties together to make a bench or stand them on their end to erect a barrier.

## ROPE AND NETTING

I couldn't quite resist the temptation to bring soccer into this somehow. Goal nets are a climber's dream—repurpose old and broken nets to give climbing plants the canvas to shine. Old roped clothesline can be tied and fastened to create a green screen overhead. Watch as a grapevine takes over. Rope and netting make such good use of vertical and overhead space to bring a whole new world of green to small and awkward spaces.

# PLASTIC BOTTLE GREENHOUSE

## GETTING STARTED

—

First you will need to construct a basic wooden frame—build one side marginally higher than the other so rain from the corrugated roof runs off. To build the walls, all you need is plastic bottles and bamboo poles. Jack used repurposed bamboo for the bottom half of his greenhouse but you can use plastic bottles from top to bottom.

Often we see greenhouses as a luxury, especially in a confined area. Such beautifully designed, heavy-duty structures offer up not only a space to grow plants but also a warm, sheltered retreat in which to have a warm drink on a cold winter's day. If you're going to opt for the top of the range, a greenhouse can set you back tens of thousands of dollars. However, what if I told you that you could create your own greenhouse considerably cheaper—and, better still, from materials that you may already have lying around in your vicinity.

Since being an avid follower of Jack (Jack's Patch on social media), it's fair to say that we've become good friends and comrades in this space of environmental and social activism. Through our common love of nature, we often find ourselves sharing techniques, experiences, and crazy ideas. On my visit to his garden, I had the pleasure of helping Jack rebuild his 8x6x7ft greenhouse made from only repurposed wood, bamboo, and 500 plastic bottles! While it should be our collective aim to end the production of single-use plastics, this project will show you how to turn single use into multiuse—thereby preventing plastics ending up in the landfill while also offering a space to grow plants and feel protected within the garden.

The beauty of a plastic bottle greenhouse is that it can be bespoke—so if you have a really small area, do not be deterred. Simply, apply the same principles shown here, but build smaller—you could even build a cold frame.

⊘  Just look at those smiles! As the clouds turned gray, Jack's bottle greenhouse not only kept the plants dry and warm, but us, too. Who knew a few bits of wood, bamboo, and bottles were all you needed.

- Lots of plastic bottles of the same size and shape (Jack collected 500 for this 8x6x7 ft greenhouse)
- Utility knife
- Bamboo poles, approx. 100, $^3/_4$ in (20 mm) longer than the height of your frame
- Jigsaw or crosscut saw
- Electric drill with $^3/_4$-in (20-mm) wood drill bit

**01**

To remove the base of each plastic bottle, hold the bottle with one hand and, using the utility knife, make a cut along any line near the base already marking the circumference of the bottle. Twist the bottle to cut all the way around.

## TO MAKE THE GUTTER

To make a gutter, saw a spare piece of repurposed bamboo in half and screw it at a downward gradient onto one of the top corners of the greenhouse frame. Repeat as needed to make a gutter trail down the side of the greenhouse frame to a water barrel positioned underneath. Use the barrel to harvest and store water from the roof. You can use a hex screw to make sure there's nothing blocking the flow of water. If you don't have bamboo, you could also use plastic guttering and secure it to the frame with brackets.

**02**

Slot the bottles together by pushing the top of one inside and up another. Do this repeatedly until you have enough bottles to fill the height of your frame.

**TIP**
—

To figure out where to make
the top and bottom holes in
the greenhouse frame to slot
the bottle bamboo poles into,
position one bottle in one
corner of the frame and one
next to it. Measure from the
center of that bottle to
the center of the next bottle
and mark these two center
points on the frame. This is
the space between holes.

### 03

With the jigsaw or crosscut saw, cut
each bamboo so it is ¾ in (20 mm)
longer than the height of the
greenhouse frame. Then feed each
bamboo through a stack of bottles
till it pokes out the top.

### 04

In order to set each bottle bamboo
pole into the frame, use the electric
drill to make a hole ⅝ in (15 mm)
deep at the top of the frame and
another ¼ in (5 mm) deep at the
bottom of the frame. Repeat for each
bottle bamboo pole (see Tip, above).

### 05

Slot a bottle bamboo pole into the
top ⅝ in (15 mm) hole in the frame
and then push it into the ¼ in (5 mm)
hole at the bottom of the frame.
Continue adding more bamboo poles
until all the bamboo poles are
securely in place.

# PALLET PLANTER

**TIP**

—

If you have a second pallet, you can repurpose the timber from that to use as the compartment bases so you don't need to measure and cut timber to fit.

Pallets are probably the most common and most glorified example of reusing materials—especially in the garden. And rightly so, they're ready-made wooden structures that hold together well and can house a whole host of ideas, solutions, and crafts. A planter on a wall, a bug hotel, a kitchen garden— I've seen it all. And what's so great is that the options are pretty much endless. You could even join pallets together to create a planted-up corner, screen, or compost bin. Or break up pallets to make planters of different shapes and sizes to create a fun green wall (or even tool storage area).

One idea is to use them to obscure eyesores: for example, to shield a trash can from view and draw the eyes to a colorful planting while still maintaining access to the trash can. Follow these steps to get your pallet planter off the ground.

## YOU WILL NEED
—

- Upcycled pallet
- Measuring tape
- 3 pieces of treated timber, measured to fit, for the compartment bases
- Pencil or pen
- Circular power saw or handsaw
- Combi drill driver
- $\frac{1}{6}$-in (4-mm) drill bit, suitable for timber
- Exterior-grade, 4mm timber screws, $1\frac{1}{2}$in (40mm) long
- Weed-proof membrane
- Heavy-duty staple gun
- $\frac{3}{8}$in (8mm) heavy-duty staples for staple gun
- Multipurpose potting mix
- Shallow-rooted plants, to go in your pallet planter

**01**

Measure the width of your pallet(s) and the width and depth of the compartment between the ground and the raised platform, which will become the planting space once it has a secure base. Mark the timber using the pencil or pen, and cut to the appropriate lengths with the saw.

**02**

Drill two 1½-in (40-mm) screws to secure the timber to the pallet blocks at each end, and in the middle, to create the compartment bases for the planter.

**03**

Staple weed membrane in the planting "pockets" to retain your soil and protect the wood.

**04**

Position the pallet in its final position, then plant up. Water generously (every day in summer) as the shallow containers will dry out quickly.

# CREATING SOWING MODULES

## YOU WILL NEED
—

- Scissors
- Toilet paper tubes
- Peat-free seed starting mix
- Watering can

What if I said you could grow peas in cardboard toilet-paper tubes? These are everyday items that can be recycled and are suitable as planters during the very first stages of a seed's life cycle. The soil in them will offer enough nutrients and space for the seeds to kick into germination. Before sowing, however, it's always best to check each seed packet for guidance, as every seed has bespoke ideal growing conditions.

Because toilet-paper tube planters are biodegradable, they can be planted directly into the ground or a larger container, once each seedling's root system is well developed. Fortunately, it really is very simple to transform a toilet paper tube into a planter (see how, opposite).

## TOILET-PAPER TUBE PLANTERS

### 01
Using scissors, cut four evenly spaced, vertical slits, ½–¾ in (1–2cm) long, at one end of a toilet paper tube.

### 02
Bend each of the four flaps back and forth, to create a crease.

### 03
Position one flap in the center of the toilet paper tube, then fold in an adjacent flap and tuck it underneath the first one. Repeat this until all four flaps lock together, to form a base to the planter.

### SOWING
For information on how to plant your seeds, see p.166.

**FROM A TOILET PAPER TUBE, THERE CAN BE LIFE—SEEING A SEED GERMINATE IN ONE NEVER FAILS TO BRING JOY**

**Recharge**
*verb*
To revive or regain energy

# RECHARGE

/ˌriːˈtʃɑːdʒ/

# I SMILE, WITNESSING THE MOSAIC OF THE FOREST

I look to the trees, seeking permission as I venture through their sacred land. They tower tall, guardians of our stories and green sanctuaries—stories otherwise lost to the winds. Guided by their dance, I wander—no destination in mind.

The trees sing symphonies. Branches and leaves chatter, whispering the occasional warning to wanderers below. Decomposing leaves crunch as ants and woodlice scatter. So still, but so full of life. I navigate roots that anchor the forest's place in the earth, treading gently, aware that any misstep might disrupt the surrounding intricate network. And so my feet communicate directly with the soil. They are part of the network of life—an extension of the amazing mycorrhizal system beneath.

As I walk deeper into the forest, sounds of society fade until they are no more. There's an instinctive alertness within, revealing itself as creatures call from the canopy above and grasses below. I watch and I listen as birds flirt and squirrels collect—I am the outsider in these parts:

everything hides upon sensing me. But I mean no harm. I wish I could tell them this.

Flies flicker and blue butterflies slow. The sun is drawing the day to a close. Amber light to pink—there's a softness to the forest now. Roaming bees catch my eye as they seek the most nectar-prized flowers. A continuous painting unfolds before me: new splashes of color emerge every second—blink and you'll miss a masterpiece. Bright pink rhododendrons energize the green landscape like fireworks in the night sky. Unfurling ferns reach out as if to welcome me into the fallen trees of the past. Their Jurassic nature makes me wonder what creatures, big and small, once voyaged through this wilderness. I brush my hand against a frond, and it bounces its approval.

An intensifying metronomic murmur distracts me. My walk becomes brisker. My curiosity needs to be sated—I cannot be stopped. Two dragonflies pirouette on a wild chase; mischievous or ominous, who knows? I come to a halt, acknowledging a slight rumbling beneath my

# MY SKIN RELISHES THE SUN, A WARMTH THAT MAKES ME FEEL AT HOME

feet. A mysterious mist is caught by the wind, refreshing my face. Water droplets are minuscule gems whipped up through the *komorebi*, and as I clear my eyes they embrace a glittering, glistening array of frolicking reflective light. There's a sudden freshness to the air as the murmuring crescendos. Then ... a stream, which cuts through the densely grown giant rhubarb, reveals itself in all its glory. All my senses are on overload.

I giggle as I compare myself to the chaotic calmness of the water and realize our connection. A leaf on a ride downstream catches my attention. The stream nudges me accordingly—I trust its direction as I wade through the pebbled water: a jigsaw of sepia hues. The pebbles—sun-seeking—catch the dappled sunlight as their shapes and sizes guide my feet. Water arcs around an ancient willow that weeps in the wind. Its wavering form hangs low as leaves tickle my feet, reassuring me on my way. After emerging through the sweep of branches, my skin relishes the sun, a warmth that makes me feel at home. I smile, witnessing the mosaic of the forest. The bountiful light bounces on the abundance of green surrounding me. I am euphoric. My mind is a maze of memories and thoughts—past, present, and future. What joy.

## In conversation with LIRA VALENCIA

Lira Valencia is a ranger for the London Wildlife Trust at a wetland in Tottenham Hale, London. On her Instagram, outsidewithlira, she encourages people to go and seek nature in urban settings.

**TAYSHAN: What's your favorite thing about nature?**

LIRA: Going out, seeking nature and finding it are, for me, a bit of a thrill.

**TAYSHAN: As someone whose mind rattles around all the time, there's this curiosity and awe that keeps me forever seeking more. Do you find that as well?**

LIRA: Yeah, wherever I am. We're so inspired by nature and don't even know it: in our music, fashion, makeup. Yesterday I found a moth that had the most beautiful colors—it was like highlighter that people apply to their cheekbones. And on the way to meet you, it was just concrete, concrete, concrete, all the way. But I was seeking. I was so upset because I didn't bring my binoculars. I was on the train thinking "I want to look out! What do normal people do when they're sitting on a train without binoculars?" I think nature keeps me present and nothing else crosses my mind.

**TAYSHAN: Walking down a road with me is a nightmare because I'm just pointing out every tree and every plant. Just being in that moment and observing what's around me rather than thinking about what's happening next. Does that happen to you, too?**

LIRA: Yeah, exactly. I think "What about right now?" especially living in a city that is so fast paced—everything is go, go, go. I think that's why I'm connected to nature because it just allows me to slow down a bit.

**TAYSHAN: I definitely struggle with that fast pace. I really struggle with structure, and I think one thing that nature isn't is structured. There are no rules.**

LIRA: That's the beauty of it. We will never know everything about nature. Throughout my whole life, I'm going to be learning something.

**TAYSHAN: It's a lifetime of learning.**

LIRA: There's so much learning to get on with, and I'm very excited.

# FOREST

# BATHING

DR. QING LI
TOKYO, JAPAN

# THE FOREST IS LIKE MY MOTHER, A SACRED PLACE, A GIFT TO ME FROM THE DIVINE. IT IS A PARADISE OF HEALING. TO STUDY THE BENEFITS OF FOREST BATHING IS MY LIFE'S WORK.

DR. QING LI

Trips to Epping Forest forever bring out my inner child. The 5,900-acre (2,400-hectare) ancient woodland straddles the border between Greater London and Essex. The name alone gives a sense of exploration, adventure, and also peace—a place to escape from the big city in search of bliss and serenity. Epping Forest, although not the closest green space to me now, occupies a very special place in my heart.

Whether it was childhood school geography trips, walking nature trails, or family days out on weekends to get us out of the house and keep my mum from exasperation, there was—and still is—a unique emotion evoked whenever entering the forest at Epping. I experience a subconscious healing of the mind, soul, and body—simply being present and immersed in nature has a profound effect, leaving me in a more clear and enriched state. It has only recently occurred to me that I've been forest bathing all my life without even knowing it.

## DID YOU KNOW?
—

Forest bathing is a Japanese practice pivoting on relaxation. It emphasizes the importance of being present, connected, and locked into your surrounding green space—acknowledging and embracing trees, plants, and wildlife. It's a practice that everyone can engage in—young and old. In Japan, it is known as *shinrin-yoku.*

## DR. QING LI'S THOUGHTS ON FOREST BATHING

We all know how good being in nature can make us feel. We have understood this for millennia. The forest sounds, the scent of the trees, the sunlight playing through the leaves, and the fresh, clean air—all these things give us a sense of comfort. They ease our stress and worry, help us relax and think more clearly. Being surrounded by nature can restore our mood, give us back our energy and vitality, as well as refresh and rejuvenate us.

We know this deep in our bones. It is like an intuition, or an instinct, a feeling that is sometimes hard to describe. In Japanese, there is a word for those feelings that are too deep for words: *yu-gen*. *Yu-gen* gives us a profound sense of the beauty and mystery of the universe. It is about this world, yet suggests something beyond it. The playwright Zeami Motokiyo describes it as the "subtle shadows of bamboo on bamboo," the feeling that you get when you "watch the sun sink behind a flower-clad hill" or "when you wander in a huge forest without thought of return."

I feel this way when I am in nature. I think of my childhood in a small village. I remember the green poplar forests in spring and summer, and the yellow leaves in the fall. I recall the games of hide and seek I played in the trees with my friends, and the animals we used to find, like rabbits and foxes, Chinese hamsters, and squirrels. There was a beautiful apricot forest in my village, which flowered pink all through April. I can still remember the taste of the apricots we harvested in the fall.

But what exactly is this feeling that is so hard to put into words? What lies behind it? How does nature make us feel this way? I am a scientist, not a poet. And I have been investigating the science behind that feeling for many years. I want to know why we feel so much better when we are in nature. What is this secret power of trees that makes us so much healthier and happier? Why is it that we feel less stressed and have more energy just by walking in a forest? Some people learn about forests. Some people study medicine. I research forest medicine to find out all the ways in which walking in a forest can improve our well-being.

## HOW TO FOREST BATHE
—

○ Switch off—turn your devices off!
○ Slow down and take in all your surroundings.
○ Engage all your senses—smell, sight, taste, sound, touch, perhaps even walk barefoot.
○ Make yourself aware of your body, its movements, and the space around it.
○ Inhale, exhale. Take in longer breaths, helping your body to relax.
○ Rest your legs by sitting down.
○ Use your eyes to observe your surroundings—the many colors, textures, and shapes of nature can soothe your mind and calm you down, especially the greens and blues.
○ Give yourself space to become one with nature.
○ Take your time—don't put any limit on your forest bathe.

## WHAT CAN YOU DO?

Forest bathing is something that we should all look to adopt as a way of life. Statistics show that we spend 90 percent of our life indoors, which is crazy. Therefore, Dr. Qing Li's work—over 30 years—dedicated to understanding the ways in which outdoor, green spaces can support our mental health and well-being is more than ever relevant now. The COVID-19 pandemic accelerated the already overwhelming mental health crisis that we face as a worldwide community. While the world went into panic, with medicine and vaccines often at the forefront of conversation, Dr. Qing Li—as the world's foremost expert in forest medicine and immunology—continued to expound on the importance of building our connection and relationship with nature. The pandemic also emphasized the value of simply being outdoors. Sadly, the Covid lockdowns disproportionately impacted those who didn't have easy access to outdoor green space.

# GROWING HERBS FOR RELAXATION

Why not grow herbs for reviving and relaxing teas or dry lavender to help soothe you to sleep? Growing your own herbs—whether you do this from seed or young plug plants—has so many benefits. Not only do they brighten up a small space and welcome wildlife, herbs bring a wealth of scent and flavor to your morning, afternoon, and evening.

## DRYING LAVENDER

When passing any lavender plant, I can't help but run my fingers through the leaves and remind myself of its smell. It immediately takes me back to my childhood home, where lavender grew in a corner of our very small garden; it was a wild bush that wasn't maintained. I often thought I'd love to somehow preserve that smell, bag it up, and take it with me. Well now I'm here to tell you that you can actually do so.

First of all, it's important to understand that lavender thrives in sun and fast-draining soil, reflecting its Mediterranean origins. Fortunately, you can grow lavender in pots, which means you have control over its drainage and its position.

The time of year that you harvest lavender is key to conserving its fragrance. Always cut lavender stems as the first flowers start to emerge. Bunch together 8–12 stems and tie with twine tightly, to prevent the flowers from falling out. Hang the lavender bunches in a dry, warm, but most importantly, well-ventilated spot. After 2–4 weeks, when the lavender flowers feel brittle, loosen each bunch and collect its blooms by gently rubbing each stem between your fingers.

Store the dried flowers in a cool, airtight container, or bag them up and keep away from light and heat, to preserve the scent and color. In this way, you really can take the fragrance of lavender around with you—whether it's in your pocket or under your pillow.

## HERBAL TEAS

The powers of tea are not to be underestimated: for warmth; for digestion; for cleansing; for its calming influence; for energy; for excitement; for medicinal use ... the list goes on. There really is a tea for any mood, place, or occasion. What's crazy to comprehend is that it's literally leaves, flowers, roots, and seeds that you're drinking—from plants that once grew in the soil, part of an ecosystem. Here I highlight a few of my personal favorite teas that you can grow yourself. Not only are all the listed plants comforting as a warm beverage, but they're also stunning plants that attract all types of wildlife and can be planted to make up a multifunctional garden. Why not grow more than one type of tea in a planter and place it conveniently near a doorway.

### BEST HERBS FOR TEA

**The calming one** Chamomile (*Chamaemelum*), likes free-draining soil and sun; use the flowers

**The explorer** Peppermint (*Mentha × piperita*), apple mint (*M. suaveolens*), spearmint (*M. spicata*), likes rich, moist soil in sun or partial shade; use the leaves

**The healer** Dog rose (*Rosa canina*), likes moist but free-draining soil in sun; use the hips

**The resilient one** Rosemary (*Salvia rosmarinus*), likes free-draining soil and sun; use the leaves

**The show off** Echinacea (*Echinacea*), likes free-draining soil and sun; use the flowers

**The soother** Lavender (*Lavandula*), likes free-draining soil and sun; use the flowers

**The versatile one** Sage (*Salvia*), likes free-draining soil and sun; use the leaves

# SENSORY PLANTS

I find it incredible that we are channeling ancient instincts everyday through what we see, what we taste, what we feel, what we smell, and what we hear. Many of my memories resurface when I experience, for example, the scents, textures, and sounds of nature. As if in a cartoon, the magic of nature transports me to moments in my life that are unlocked in an instant.

Suddenly, walking along a path or down a road becomes an adventure where sight steers, smells soothe, and sound guides. I find that living through my senses changes my perspectives, evokes special feelings, and heightens my taste buds. Perhaps you might find the same if you include some of these plants in your garden. I spotted them on a sensory walk in my community.

## SMELL
### LAVENDER (*LAVANDULA*)

The floral, herbal, and woodsy fragrances of lavender massage the mind, body, and soul. Its relaxing properties are captured in myriad herbal products, and you can also enjoy it when you brush your hands around lavender flowers in full bloom. It reminds me of my mum in many ways: in her garden; in a lavender diffuser in her bedroom, and as an oil in her baths.

## SIGHT
### PHEASANT'S TAIL GRASS (*ANEMANTHELE LESSONIANA*)

This is one of my favorite grasses for its multi-tone leaf textures as exuberant greens turn to fall reds. Its foliage also dances in the wind and glistens in the sun. Although not an obvious choice to capture the eye, its elegance softens the landscape and the mind. Pheasant's tail could be used in a prairie-style palette and complements colorful perennials such as coneflowers (both *Rudbeckia* and *Echinacea*) and purple tops (*Verbena bonariensis*).

142

## SOUND
### BLACK BAMBOO
### (*PHYLLOSTACHYS NIGRA*)

Being immersed in black bamboo can teleport you across the universe. Its evergreen leaves and lustrous black canes (stems) rustle in the wind, and they can warn of incoming rain and stormy weather, too. Black bamboo is tall in stature, reaching 13 ft (4 m) or more high, and offers year-round green screening. This woody-stemmed, rhizomatous perennial is low maintenance and is generally clump-forming in a cool-temperate climate.

## TOUCH
### LAMB'S EAR
### (*STACHYS BYZANTINA*)

The white-woolly, gray-green leaves are the softest to touch, so this plant is called lamb's ear for a very good reason. It's crazy that this is a plant that just grows out of the ground—it feels like something you could throw on instantly to keep you warm and comfy on a cold day (you'd need quite a few leaves). This mat-forming perennial is also known for its culinary and medicinal properties.

## TASTE
### WILD GARLIC
### (*ALLIUM URSINUM*)

Wild garlic, also known as ramson, is something I discovered quite recently and since then has been added to ingredients I love to use when cooking. It's often found abundantly in woodland, so there's no denying that it's a forager's favorite. The edible leaves, while distinctively garlicky, are noticeably light in taste and can be added as a seasoning to pesto, soups, and savory dishes.

# STORAGE SEAT

**VARIATION**
—

If you want more storage
space, why not add hinges
and a lid to the back
planter. You can then use
it as storage space instead
of growing plants there.

A place to relax, a place to share, a place to eat, a place to
chat ... a place to pause for a second. The opportunity to sit
down should not be underestimated—it offers the chance to
take the weight off your feet as well as off your mind.

This storage seat is an opportunity to make something
bespoke, personal, and perfect for you and your space. Maybe,
it will be a seat to take in a special view? A multipurpose space
to store outdoor/garden items in a small area? Or possibly you'd
like to green up a spot with wildlife-friendly planting? This
storage seat does all of these things.

When you look at this storage seat as a whole, it might feel
a bit complex. However, all it really entails is building three
planters with a seat that sits comfortably around them. Choose
the type of wood you'd like to use and see if you can repurpose
some—we've selected decking board. If you have the space,
I'd advise building 6 ft (1.8 m) wide (as I have here) so your
bench can seat 2–3 people—it's always nice to sit and share a
moment with family or a friend. The outer planters are the same
height, width, and depth, while the back planter is considerably
longer. Try to find level ground to situate your seat—if necessary,
position offcuts beneath the planters until it is level side to side
and front to back before step 10.

⊙ Creating spaces to sit
in the garden is just
as important as
having room to move
around in it. Why not
put up your feet and
relax for a bit? A
2-in-1, this bench
also shelters tools
and pots beneath.

## YOU WILL NEED
—

- Measuring tape
- Pencil or pen
- Circular power saw or handsaw
- Combi drill driver
- $\frac{1}{6}$-in (4-mm) wood drill bit
- Screwdriver bits for drill
- Carpenter's try square
- Weed-proof membrane, 33 ft (10 m) long and 6$\frac{1}{2}$ ft (2 m) wide
- Heavy-duty staple gun and $\frac{3}{8}$-in (8-mm) heavy-duty staples
- Multipurpose, peat-free potting mix
- Plants, to fit the planter

### Screws

- Exterior-grade, 4mm timber screws, 1$\frac{1}{2}$in (40mm) long
- Exterior-grade, 4mm timber screws, 2in (50mm) long
- Exterior-grade, 4.5mm timber screws, 2$\frac{1}{2}$in (60mm) long
- Exterior-grade, 5mm timber screws, 3in (80mm) long

### For the two side planters

- 20 panels, 32in (800mm) long, of decking board, 4$\frac{3}{4}$×$\frac{3}{4}$in (120×20mm), for the sides
- 20 panels, 12in (300mm) long, of decking board, 4$\frac{3}{4}$×$\frac{3}{4}$in (120×20mm), for the front and back
- 14 panels, 12in (300mm) long, of decking board, 4$\frac{3}{4}$×$\frac{3}{4}$in (120×20mm), for the base
- 8 support posts, 18in (450mm) long, of treated timber, 1$\frac{1}{4}$×1$\frac{1}{4}$in (32×32mm)

### For the back planter

- 10 panels, 48in (1,200mm) long, of decking board, 4$\frac{3}{4}$×$\frac{3}{4}$in (120×20mm), for the sides
- 10 panels, 16in (400mm) long, of decking board, 4$\frac{3}{4}$×$\frac{3}{4}$in (120×20mm), for the front and back
- 3 panels, 48in (1,200mm) long, of decking board, 4$\frac{3}{4}$×$\frac{3}{4}$in (120×20mm), for the base
- 6 support posts, 18in (450mm) long, of treated timber, 1$\frac{1}{4}$×1$\frac{1}{4}$in (32×32mm)

### For the seat

- 3 bench supports, 13$\frac{3}{4}$in (350mm) long, of treated timber, 2×2in (50×50mm)
- 5 bench legs, at least 13$\frac{3}{4}$in (350mm) long, of treated timber, 2×2in (50×50mm)
- 3 seat panels, 48in (1,200mm) long, of decking board, 4$\frac{3}{4}$×$\frac{3}{4}$in (120×20mm)
- 2 side seat rails, 13$\frac{1}{2}$in (340mm) long, of treated timber, 1$\frac{1}{4}$×1$\frac{1}{4}$in (32×32mm)
- 1 middle seat rail, 11$\frac{1}{2}$in (290mm) long, of treated timber, 1$\frac{1}{4}$×1$\frac{1}{4}$in (32×32mm)

## 01

Measure the space you'd like your bench to fit into. The space I built in was 4 ft (1.2 m) wide and 32 in (80 cm) deep. The height of my five panels of decking board, 4¾ x ¾ in (120 x 20 mm), was 24 in (600 mm). Cut the timber to length (or, if you have the budget, you can sometimes pay for precut wood).

## 02

Drill two pilot holes into both ends of all the panels—bar one panel from each set. The remaining panels will be the top ones around the planter and need pilot holes drilled at the bottom of each end, then a second hole in the middle between the base hole and the top of each panel.

## HEALTH AND SAFETY
—

Gloves, ear protectors, and eye protection are recommended when cutting and drilling into wood.

### 03

To build a side planter, line up four 32-in (800-mm) panels and position a support post underneath at each end. Drill 1½-in (40-mm) screws through your pilot holes to secure the panels to the post. Screw a fifth panel in place at the top—this panel overlaps the top of the post. This forms one side of the planter.

### 04

Use the try square to line up a 12-in (300-mm) front/back panel (you can rest it on top of something to make sure the height is level). Screw all five front/back panels into the support posts to create an L shape, using 1½-in (40-mm) screws.

### 05

Repeat step 03 to make the second side. Then line it up with the short side and screw in place. Drill five more front/back panels at the other end. Use the 1½-in (40-mm) screws. Repeat steps 03–05 to build the second side planter.

## 06

Turn each side planter upside down and screw the base panels in place, using the 1½-in (40-mm) screws.

## 07

To create the back planter, follow steps above but with the appropriate different cuts of wood. On the long edge, measure and mark the halfway point—this is where you will secure two additional posts in the middle for support on both sides.

## 08

Then drill additional pilot holes at the marked halfway points at the top and bottom of each panel and affix a support post to it, using the 1½-in (40-mm) screws.

**09**

**09**

Join the three planters together by affixing 3-in (80-mm) screws through post to post. Where a post backs onto only a panel, screw from the panel side using 1½-in (40-mm) screws.

**10**

Line each planter with a weed-proof membrane and secure to the wood with the staple gun. Inside the enclosure, draw a line 14–16 in (35–40 cm) from the ground and use the spirit level to make sure the line is parallel to the ground. Using 2½-in (60-mm) screws, secure the three bench supports so each top face aligns with the marked line. Then measure from the bottom of the bench supports down to the ground. This is how you find the lengths you need to cut each bench leg; these may all differ depending on ground levels. Affix these to the planter with 3-in (80-mm) screws (where leg posts can screw into planter support posts) and 2½-in (60-mm) screws (where you can screw only into a planter side panel)—one at each end of the side planter bench supports and one in the middle of the back planter bench support.

**10**

## 11

Take the seat panels and place them upside down, resting them on top of the bench supports, leaving a small gap between each to allow rain to run off. The bench should sit snug on this ridge. (We did this so we could screw in the seat rails from above before affixing the seat in place.) Loosely place 2 x 2-in (50 x 50-mm) offcuts flush against the sides and back. This will help you position the seat rails away from where the bench supports are. Use the 2-in (50-mm) screws to secure the seat rails to the three seat panels (one at each side and one along the middle). You can then discard any loose offcuts. Flip the seat over from right to left.

## 12

With the 2½-in (60-mm) screws, drill through the seat rails into the bench supports under the seat (one at the front and one at the back) to affix it in place.

## 13

Fill each planter with potting mix, leaving a ¾-in (2-cm) gap from the top, to allow for watering. Then plant up.

/ˌrev.əˈluː.ʃən.aɪz/

# REVOLUTIONIZE

**revolutionize**
verb
to bring about a radical or
fundamental change

# "THEY BURIED US.

# THEY DIDN'T KNOW

# WE WERE SEEDS."

**DINOS CHRISTIANOPOULOS**

## PLANTING SEEDS OF CHANGE

Timing is everything—you need to know when to plant your seeds. While germinating, they are delicate and are at their most vulnerable stage in their life cycle. Some of the most important things to bear in mind are to:

> ensure the ground in which you are planting the seeds is both suitable and fertile; you might have appropriate seed, but you might be sowing it in the wrong place;
> water your seed and remember that growth isn't always visible—the roots will be doing the very important anchoring beneath the surface while you wait;
> nurture your seedling as it emerges; always give it constant love and light to ensure it receives all the nutrients needed;
> embrace and enjoy its growth—watch the seed that you planted flourish;
> realize that there will always be failures and difficulties to overcome, but they will help your seedling become more resilient.

There's something symbolic about the growth of a seed—its resilience, its adaptability, the hope. There are lessons that reveal themselves throughout cycles of life. We are nature and nature is us.

I'm always torn when aligning my life's journey, my experiences, and now my work, to the word "revolution." Since first being dubbed the Grenfell Guerrilla Gardener, after I had first put spade to ground in 2017, my idea of the word has evolved. It's important to put my changing perceptions into context and to understand the background landscape: the COVID-19 pandemic and its continuing global impact; the cost-of-living crisis hitting hard in the most deprived areas; the Grenfell Tower fire in 2017 on my doorstep and close to my heart; and losing my mother in 2020 to cancer ....

From my involvement in guerrilla gardening and on to Grow to Know, you can't help but think that what I and my friends are doing is revolutionary: it's different; it challenges norms; and it brings about much-needed change. You might see our actions as radical; you might see them as revolutionary—but I will always argue that they need to be and should be the norm. It's time to flip the script. Yes—we're addressing and confronting massive social and environmental injustices, but what is the alternative? What's so different about what we're doing? What exactly are we confronting? What are we changing? Quite simply, how did we get to this point?

The answers to some of these questions might just help us to understand how close, or far, we are from achieving as unified and positive an outcome as possible. Many factors influence what we all believe, and what is true to us as individuals. Our experiences, privileges, and disadvantages all play a big part in what we believe to be true. This could be said about pretty much anything in society, but, as my late mother would say, surely we must start by communicating, engaging, and understanding better.

Here are some questions to challenge you to start rethinking your priorities in life:

> Do you think we're becoming further disconnected from nature? How important to you is our connection to nature and each other?
> Do you believe our education system and curriculum are outdated? Do you think that nature should be at the forefront and foundation of education?
> Do you consider growing your own food to be a radical act? Would you grow your own food if you could?
> Do you think creating wider access to green space is revolutionary? Do you have immediate access to any green space?
> Is community important to you? Do you feel part of a community?

## THE COMMON GROUND

I've spent a lot of time reflecting on my thoughts and emotions, as well as on what's worked in both past and present, and where I position myself in all of this.

When you personally think about revolution, you might concentrate on a fight, a war, or battles—and, don't get me wrong, at times I've been at war with the world and, even more so,

# SURELY WE MUST START BY COMMUNICATING, ENGAGING, AND UNDERSTANDING BETTER

with myself. What if revolution is about respect, unity, and deeper understanding? Isn't that fundamental to solution seeking? Shouldn't that be what drives us? It's definitely what motivates me—please hear me out ...

I've realized just how powerful nature can be. I've seen it light up the eyes of young and old; I've noticed it bring people together at a time of need ... it has saved me. Nature is what I like to call the common ground. Gardens, parks, plots, rooftops, playgrounds, and even windowsills—nature is emotive, it's poetic, it's every day, it's part of life. We are nature.

Whether you're the president, prime minister, in prison, or in primary school, you're almost definitely going to have at least some shared views on how the weather makes you feel, or how seeing a butterfly makes you smile, or how you appreciate a particular tree—I can guarantee it. Thus, revolution for me is really about honing in on and creating avenues of discussion that pivot on that common ground—similar, shared, or even differing views and experiences of nature. Essentially, it's the way to provide fertile ground for healthy discussion and collective understanding and action, and to plant seeds in the ground and in minds.

Grow to Know's appearance at RHS Chelsea Flower Show 2022 exemplifies just how this approach could work (see p.14). And so, yes—maybe the radical part is trying to change some of those systems that oppress opportunities for positive engagement in society and the environment in general.

I made my entrance into this space as an activist, which then opened my mind up as I've stepped into a career as a gardener, which soon became entrepreneurial. I was an activist before I even knew what the word meant; I was an entrepreneur before I even knew what the word meant; I was a horticulturalist before I even knew what the word meant. My point is, I don't claim to understand it all, nor do I pretend to be perfect. I don't have all the answers. But the clue is in the word "activist": I take action, I try, I fail, and I always seek opportunities to listen, to reflect, and to learn. It's the failures that I really am starting to appreciate—they used to catch me by surprise, but I've grown this resilience that has really aided my progress.

We must be able to adapt, flex, and maneuver through difficulty. This is something I'm still working on daily, and it's a challenging process, especially with the continuous pressures felt. It is so vital that we reconnect, rethink, regenerate, reimagine, rewild, repurpose, and recharge.

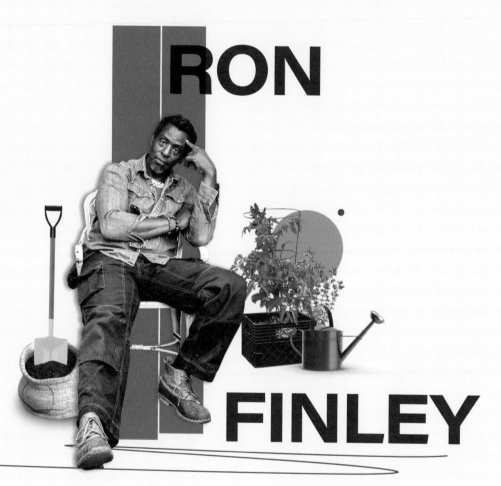

# RON
# FINLEY

THE RON FINLEY PROJECT
LOS ANGELES

"If kids plant broccoli, they eat broccoli. If kids plant tomatoes, they eat tomatoes."

Simple but wise words from my brother Ron Finley. How could you argue with them?

Ron continued, "Let shovels be the weapons of choice and seeds be the ammo."

These words were soon to touch screens worldwide as Ron told his story of urban gardening in his community, attempting to introduce homegrown, natural foods to the people in his TED talk. A guerrilla garden that Ron planted in 2010 brought discussion on gardening, knowledge, and togetherness to the forefront. Little did we know that Ron and I started off on similar paths, but just on the other side of the "pond" ...

By the time my friends and I were planting seeds in a wide range of unloved spaces in North Kensington, just after the Grenfell Tower fire, Ron's previously derelict patch at the side of a road in South Central Los Angeles had become a sanctuary for the local community. There, fruit

and vegetables came to yield as neighbors lent a hand, and families came and ate.

Soon after receiving a penalty notice from the City of Los Angeles for planting a food forest on the "dirt patch" outside his front door, Ron and a few fellow activists came together to fight back. A petition was set up, and this resulted in the council waiving enforcement of a city law that required sidewalks to be free from obstruction; from then on, vegetable gardens designed for community use were to be permitted. This came to be the start of Ron's horticultural revolution. He would use it to inspire people to get gardening.

## What can you do?

Ron's commitment is infectious. He believes you need a balance between realizing the here-and-now and counting your blessings, while also understanding the part you have to play in the bigger picture and the ripples of the future. Some things you can do are: manifest, plan, plot, scheme, action, and mobilize. Get together, get talking, get growing. Start off by planting one seed, one plant, one tree, and see what happens. What space can you take over?

Gathering context and perspective is just as important, whether that's on a personal level, geographic, economic, societal, or environmental. Seek and search for what was, what is, and what could be ... and, most importantly, question everything—even if just to yourself, because the real revolution truly begins within.

# GROWING YOUR OWN FOOD IS LIKE PRINTING YOUR OWN MONEY
**RON FINLEY**

# In conversation with
# RON FINLEY

Ron is a real pioneer—not just for the action he takes, but also because of the narrative he pushes, his choice of language, and the perceptions he shares to shift culture. Here, we reflect on the revolution that we play a part in.

**TAYSHAN: For people who aren't aware of your journey into guerrilla gardening, please could you give a bit of context?**

RON: I don't do guerrilla gardening— I do gangster gardening. When I was growing up, it would be like, "Man, that's gangster." It was a way to say that something was cool.

**TAYSHAN: And do you see what you're doing as also being revolutionary?**

RON: What I do is akin to freedom. Yeah, it's revolutionary, but only because other people have set up artificial constraints.

**TAYSHAN: For younger people growing up, who maybe don't think that gardening is gangster, how do we change that?**

RON: It needs to be taught in kindergarten. It needs to be taught in the first grade; it needs to be taught in junior high. It needs to be taught in senior high; it needs to be taught in college. This is a life skill. This ain't no hobby. Everyone needs to know how to feed themselves. If kids are shown the value of so-called rubbish being turned into compost, we'd have them growing food from such "waste." So when they grow up, they're gonna look at waste as a resource; they're gonna look at it as money. I think we would be creating a whole generation of environmental entrepreneurs.

**TAYSHAN: And what's the one thing you would pick out in your garden?**

RON: One of the things that brings me joy is when people come and they say, "It's amazing." But, to me, it's not.

**TAYSHAN: I guess for some people it takes a lot of resources that they don't have to find spaces that make them go "wow." What you are showing, and what I find in London, is that we're creating those access points. Some kid that lives on the 20th floor of a block can see someone who grew up in the same area doing something that they never thought was possible—in the same way that I wanted to be a footballer [soccer player] growing up, because I knew people around me who did that. But gardening was never sold to us in that way, and it needs to be rebranded and remarketed.**

RON: That's my whole thing. How do we make gardening sexy? All this gangster rap ain't gangster. Gardening's gangster—you're changing people's lives.

# SEED BOMBING

## YOU WILL NEED
—

- multipurpose potting mix
- Flour
- Bowl
- Water
- Packet of native wildflower seed mix or vegetable seeds

Have you ever wondered if you could bring a garden along with you in your pocket? Let me introduce you to the seed bomb— a firework of flowers or vegetables ready to explode into life. Just like fireworks, there's no guarantee that the seeds will germinate and subsequently burst into color, but when they do you just have to admire them in awe—they make seed bombs so worthwhile.

Seed bombs are often a guerrilla gardener's weapon of choice, because they are an easy and quick way of accelerating the process of seed dispersal—in a similar way to animals and wind distributing seeds. By using a seed bomb filled with the seeds of your choice you can adopt a naturalistic, experimental, and playful approach to gardening—rewilding a space while also reclaiming the idea of what a gardener is and what a garden looks like. Although the process of germination is one that takes time and patience, there are ways you can encourage it and take action almost instantly with very little prep needed. Find out how to make your own seed bombs here. It's a great activity to do with kids!

**01**
Mix 10 parts potting mix to one part flour in a bowl.

**02**
Slowly add water until the mixture has a sticky, doughlike consistency and molds together.

**03**
Add the wildflower or vegetable seeds so they are evenly scattered throughout the mixture.

**04**
Roll a clump of the soil mixture into a golf-ball shape between the palms of your hands. Make further, similarly shaped balls until all the soil mixture has been used.

**05**
Leave the seed balls to dry for a couple of days. Then throw them in spaces of your choice.

# A FIREWORK OF FLOWERS
# OR VEGETABLES READY
# TO EXPLODE INTO LIFE

# GROWING SKILLS

To get the best results from the challenge of regreening small spaces in your area, it is important to understand the basics of plant care.

## The importance of aspect

Knowing how much sun or shade your chosen site receives is essential in order to grow plants successfully. To thrive, some plants require a hot, sunny position, while others prefer partial or full shade. Therefore, you need to choose plants that suit these places. Individual parts of the site may also have different climatic conditions: for example, by being exposed to wind turbulence or by being protected by a warm wall. Such microclimates should also be borne in mind when planting.

## Soils and potting mixes

The degree of acidity or alkalinity (pH) in soil affects what plants can be grown. A pH below 7 (which is neutral) indicates acid soil, while a pH above 7 means alkaline soil. The pH level for optimum plant growth is between 5.5 and 7.5. Although many plants tolerate a wide pH range, there are some that prefer a particular soil type: sandy, silty, or clay. Sandy soils are very light, free-draining, and acidic. Silty soils are more fertile, retain moisture better, and tend to have a more neutral pH. Clay soils are heavier, more alkaline, rich in nutrients, and retain moisture well. To check your soil, buy a soil testing kit from your local garden center. Ordinary garden soil (loam) should

not be used in pots, troughs, or any other type of container, because it might contain weed seeds and disease spores. Instead, use multipurpose potting mixes, either loamless ones or loam-based ones. Loamless potting mixes, which should be peat-free, are suitable for short-term use, such as sowing seeds and growing young plants. Being relatively lightweight, they should also be used in hanging baskets and for containers on rooftop gardens and balconies. Loam-based potting mixes are heavier, less prone to waterlogging, and provide a steady supply of nutrients, so they are good for long-term planting. Acid-loving plants will need ericaceous potting mix.

## Basic tools

The most important gardening tools are a trowel, a hand fork, a pair of pruners, and a watering can (for this, you can repurpose any container with a spout). For a large area, a garden fork and garden spade will also be invaluable. Always keep your tools clean, sharp, and in good condition.

## When to plant

Although container-grown plants can be planted year-round, they establish more quickly if planted at the start of the growing season, in spring, or in fall, when the soil is still warm from the summer heat.

## How to plant

Before planting, clear the ground of any large stones and all weeds. Then feed the soil with organic matter such as manure or garden compost. Also, water the plant or plants well, so they are fully hydrated.

For each plant, dig a hole twice the width of its root ball and a little deeper. With a fork, loosen around the edges and base of the planting hole. Add a handful of organic material to the planting hole, then water it. Remove the plant from its pot and gently tease out the roots before placing it in the planting hole at the same depth that it was in its pot; this is indicated by a dark mark on the stem. Backfill with the soil and firm gently. Finally, water the plant again, to settle the soil around the roots.

Repeat for any second and subsequent plant, spacing them so they will not crowd each other once fully mature. If sowing seeds, follow spacing and planting depth on the packet.

## Container tips

When selecting a container, bear in mind that it should be large enough to hold sufficient potting soil to feed the plant as it develops, and that it should also have good drainage holes.

Containers are available in a range of shapes, materials, and finishes: plastic is lightweight and the most versatile material, because it can be molded into a wide variety of shapes, but it does become brittle with age. Traditional clay unglazed pots are heavier and have more character, but may not be frost proof. Being porous, they keep plants cooler in summer than non-porous plastic containers; they require more watering, though.

Before planting, scrub the container thoroughly to ensure it is clean. To enhance drainage, place a layer of crocks (pieces of broken pots) or chunks of polystyrene in the base of the container. Partially fill the container with potting soil (see Soils and potting mixes, above), then add the plant (or plants) so they are sitting at the same level as in their previous pots. Backfill with potting soil around each plant and firm in, so that the potting soil is about 2 in (5 cm) from the rim. Water the plant well.

## Caring for your plants

To keep your plants in peak condition you need to take care of them throughout the year. One of the main tasks is to water them regularly, especially if they are recently germinated seedlings and other young plants. You will also have to water plants more often in hot, dry weather. Container-grown plants require more watering than those growing directly in the ground. Always water plants when evaporation will be low, that is in the early morning or in the evening.

Once established, most plants benefit from being fed every spring with well-rotted manure, garden compost, or an organic pelleted or granular fertilizer, while container-grown plants need more regular feeding, with liquid fertilizer.

To encourage more blooms, deadhead flowers regularly unless decorative seed heads are required or the seed is to be collected once ripe.

Weeds compete with your ornamental plants for moisture and nutrients, so pull them out of the soil or potting mix as soon as convenient.

At the start of the growing season, remove each container-grown plant from its pot so you can check that its roots are healthy and that the plant has not outgrown its container and become pot-bound. If appropriate, replant it in fresh potting mix in a container that is marginally larger (up to 2 in/5 cm more in diameter) than the previous one, so the plant has room to develop further (see How to plant, p.167).

Some plants will need supporting as they develop. For example, tall perennials and shrubs with weak stems require propping up, preferably with well-branched twigs or canes but otherwise with metal stakes. Train climbers up trellis or wires, and tie them in at regular intervals using string tied in a figure-eight knot.

## Pruning

The main tasks when pruning a plant are to remove all dead, dying, and diseased stems, to improve the plant's health and vigor. Then weak, straggly, over-vigorous, and crossing stems should be cut out, to leave a strong, well-balanced framework.

## Troubleshooting

The best way to avoid problems is to choose plants that are adapted to the type of conditions in your garden (see The importance of aspect, p.166, and Soils and potting mixes, p.166) and to grow them in a biodiverse environment, where beneficial creatures such as bugs, bees, ladybugs, and worms are encouraged. Also, always pay attention to your plant's everyday needs (see Caring for your plants, p.167). Strong, healthy plants are better able to fend off pests and diseases than those that are struggling. If your plant does start to wilt, or its foliage becomes discolored or otherwise damaged, try to revive it by soaking it in a bucket of water for 30 minutes or so; then leave to drain. If the plant fails to recover, check its roots, stems, and leaves for signs of pest or disease damage. Remove any pests by hand; avoid using chemicals, to protect the environment. Never put a diseased plant in the compost heap.

# BIBLIOGRAPHY

**Reconnect**
**015–016 Hands Off Mangrove** Mangrove Nine Protest, nationalarchives.gov.uk/education/resources/mangrove-nine-protest/ **015–016 Hands Off Mangrove** Saunders, S., "The Mangrove Nine", Anti Racist Cumbria, 2021

**Rethink**
**031 Did You Know?** "Food systems account for over one-third of global greenhouse gas emissions", United Nations, 2021

**Regenerate**
**048–049 The Mushroom Movement** Viana, C., "Benefits of Fungi for the Environment and Humans", Chloride Free, 2021 **049 Human Health (edible mushroom data)** Marshall, E. and Nair, N. G., "Make money by growing mushrooms" report, Food and Agriculture Organization of the United Nations, 2009 **067 Maruvan (Japanese forest data)** Wikipedia: Akira Miyawaki **067 Did You Know?** www.sugiproject.com/about **068 Rajasthan, India – Maruvan** www.sugiproject.com/projects/maruvan

**Reimagine**
**075 Did You Know?** "Mental Health and Our Changing Climate: Impacts, Implications, and Guidance", The American Psychological Association and ecoAmerica, 2017 **079 Bosco Verticale (planting data)** Xie, J., "High-rise forests in Italy are fighting air pollution", The Verge, 2017

**079 Bosco Verticale (carbon data)** Horton, B. A., Wright, R., "Welcome to the Milan apartments where 300 humans live in harmony with 21,000 trees", Euronews, 2021 **082 Plant Your Own Pollution Barrier (premature deaths data)** Dajnak, D., Evangelopoulos, D., Kitwiroon, N., Beevers, S., Walton, H., "London Health Burden Of Current Air Pollution And Future Health Benefits Of Mayoral Air Quality Policies", Imperial College London, 2021 **087–088 Brooklyn Grange** www.brooklyngrangefarm.com **093 Did You Know?** Corfe, S., "What are the barriers to eating healthily in the UK?", Social Market Foundation, 2018

**Rewild**
**103 The High Line** www.thehighline.org **104 What Can You Do?** "Essential maintenance work on the A40 Westway", Transport for London press release, 2021 **105 Table** www.thehighline.org/blog/2021/09/14/plants-and-insects/

**Recharge**
**137 Quote** From *Shinrin-Yoku* by Dr Qing Li, published by Penguin, Copyright © Dr Qing Li, 2018, Reprinted by permission of Penguin Books Limited **138 Dr Qing Li's Thoughts on Forest Bathing (excerpt)** From *Shinrin-Yoku* by Dr Qing Li, published by Penguin, Copyright © Dr Qing Li, 2018, Reprinted by permission of Penguin Books Limited

# INDEX

# ACKNOWLEDGMENTS

I can't express just how blessed I feel to be surrounded by inspiring, supportive, and kind people. Writing this book has deepened my understanding of myself: my identity and purpose in the wider context of the world. At times, I really heard peoples' concern and worry, but also appreciated and channeled their brilliance, resilience, and wisdom.

Firstly, I would like to thank my two children, Luca Blu and Jazz Rae. They often find themselves tagging along to the office or to a project. Sometimes, at home, I might be so engaged in work they won't be able to even get a word in. I'm super aware of the importance of being a present and positive role model to you. Admittedly, there has been and will be a lot of sacrifice. I just hope that one day it will all make sense and it will be worth it. It's fair to say that your patience, understanding, and love is reassuring and often keeps me going. At the crux of this is Opal, who has been a rock during the hardest times—who has been that hands-on parent whilst also juggling life's many challenges. You are appreciated. I would also like to thank and acknowledge my younger siblings, Tibiyan and Leo, who feel the pressures of life but still take everything in their strides as they grow and flower—there's so much yet to come. Thank you Auntie Petra, Compton, Helen, Liz, as well as the many parents and others who continue to do their best to offer support and love in the absence of my mum.

A common theme of my thanks and appreciation is the patience and understanding of those around me— it is no secret that I don't always have everything together. Massive appreciation for the support, flexibility, and constant motivation that Lucy Philpott and Tania Gomes have continually shown me throughout. It has been a pleasure to get to know you both and be on this journey with such kind and wholesome people. A special thank you to team DK— Chris Young, Katie Cowan, and Ruth O'Rourke (and everyone else!) for putting trust in me and for being nothing but real and supportive.

This book is all about collaboration: from Alex Cunningham who helped massively with the build of many projects; Sal Chebbah who teaches me something new everyday about mushrooms; Jack Hodgson who is the king of repurposing, creating, and crafting; to Sebastian Barros for capturing the journey so emotively and authentically.

Thank you to my agent, Jan Croxson and Borra Garson (and the rest of the amazing team DML) for your guidance, words of advice, and for helping me to take steps into unfamiliar territory with confidence and with pride—I appreciate you.

A big up to everyone who has contributed to the book, offering perspectives, insights, and stories which just showcase the beauty of diversity, culture, and nature. Chats with my good friends, colleagues, and heroes—Danny Clarke, Tom Massey, Lira Valencia, George Lamb, and Ron Finley—have given me hope and make me so proud to stand in power amongst such inspiring comrades. Thank you to the people and organizations who have offered us a glimpse into their work: GROW in Totteridge, Joshua Kwaku Asiedu in Ghana, Charles Dowding in Somerset, SUGi projects worldwide, Milan's Bosco Verticale, New York's Brooklyn Grange Farm and High Line, Jens Jakobsen in London, Dr. Qing Li in Tokyo, and Ron Finley in LA.

I also appreciate the help from the many unnamed friends and colleagues who have been a sounding board, a second pair of eyes, and a pool of knowledge whenever I've had questions, thoughts, or ideas.

I would also like to thank activists, campaigners, and innovators—past and present—who put energy and time into creating a better and beautiful future. I write this in 2023 when there are so many injustices, from wars to Grenfell tower, and from climate change to social challenges which are often faced by the most marginalized people. I hope for a day when we don't have to fight for joy.

Finally, thank you Mum for giving me the tools, the compassion, and fighting spirit you so gracefully shared with me in the 23 years we spent together in the physical world.

Big love to all, Tayshan.

# ABOUT THE AUTHOR

Tayshan Hayden-Smith is an activist, changemaker, community gardener, community organizer, and passionate believer in people's right to have access to nature and joy. Formerly a professional soccer player, he sought to heal and inspire hope in his North Kensington community following the tragedy of the Grenfell Tower fire by initiating the Grenfell Garden of Peace. Since focusing on his gardening and activism, he now runs his own nonprofit company Grow to Know. Tayshan is also part of the design team on BBC2's Your Garden Made Perfect, and his garden at RHS Chelsea Flower Show 2022 won a Silver Gilt medal.

## PUBLISHER'S ACKNOWLEDGMENTS

The publisher would like to thank Alex Cunningham for work on the Root Window Planter, Keyhole Raised Bed, Compost Bin, Food Ladder, Pollinator Wall, Pallet Planter, and Storage Seat; Sal Chebbah for work on Grow Your Own Mushrooms; and Jack Hodgson for work on the Plastic Bottle Greenhouse. DK would also like to thank Danny Clarke, George Lamb, Tom Massey, Lira Valencia, and Ron Finley for their conversations with Tayshan. Also, thanks to Meanwhile Gardens Community Association and St. Clements and St. James CofE Primary School for accommodating photo shoots, Jackie Swanson for the picture research, Alice McKeever for the proofread, and Lisa Footitt for the index.

## PICTURE CREDITS

The publisher would like to thank the following for their kind permission to reproduce their photographs:
(Key: a-above; b-below/bottom; c-centre; f-far; l-left; r-right; t-top)

**14 Alamy Stock Photo:** Guy Bell / Alamy Live News (1/c, 3/c); Michael Preston (2/c). **15 Sebatian Barros**. **16 Alamy Stock Photo:** Guy Bell / Alamy Live News (bl). **17 Sebatian Barros**. **20 Shutterstock.com:** Hurst Photo (tl). **28 GROW:** Helena Dolby (3); we are GROW (1); Leonie Freeman (2). **29 GROW:** Leonie Freeman (t). **31 GROW:** Laura Aziz (b); Helena Dolby (t). **38 Joshua Kwaku Asiedu:** Joshua Kwaku Asiedu (2, 1). **40 Joshua Kwaku Asiedu:** Joshua Kwaku Asiedu. **41 Joshua Kwaku Asiedu:** Joshua Kwaku Asiedu. **43 Shutterstock.com:** Hurst Photo. **50 Shutterstock.com:** Nick Harvey. **52 Charles Dowding:** Jonathan Buckley (1) (2, 3). **53 Charles Dowding:** . **54 Charles Dowding:** Jonathan Buckley (br). **55 Charles Dowding:** Edward Dowding. **56 Shutterstock.com:** Hurst Photo. **66 Maruvan Foundation:** (1, 2). **67 Maruvan Foundation**. **68 Maruvan Foundation**. **69 Maruvan Foundation:** (b, t). **71 Shutterstock.com:** Hurst Photo. **78 Alamy Stock Photo:** mauritius images GmbH. **79 Alamy Stock Photo:** Claudio Giovanni Colombo. **80 Unsplash:** Daniel Sessler. **81 Alamy Stock Photo:** UMB-O. **82 Shutterstock.com:** Hurst Photo. **83 Shutterstock.com:** Hurst Photo. **84 Dorling Kindersley:** Mark Winwood / RHS Wisley (br, tr). **85 Dorling Kindersley:** Mark Winwood / RHS Chelsea Flower Show 2014 (tl); Mark Winwood / RHS Wisley (tr, bl, tc). **86 Alamy Stock Photo:** AP Photo / Seth Wenig. **87 Getty Images:** Carolyn Cole-Los Angeles Times. **88 Alamy Stock Photo:** AP Photo / Seth Wenig (b); Jan Traylen (t). **89 Alamy Stock Photo:** AP Photo / Seth Wenig. **92 Shutterstock.com:** Hurst Photo. **93 Alamy Stock Photo:** A Garden. **100 Wax London:** Jack Batchelor. **102 Alamy Stock Photo:** Michael Gamblin / Alamy Stock Photo (1); Ray Warren Creative (3); Kristin Lee Photo (2). **103 Alamy Stock Photo:** Richard Green. **104 Alamy Stock Photo:** Patti McConville. **106 Shutterstock.com:** Hurst Photo. **109 Shutterstock.com:** Hurst Photo. **116 Jens Jakobsen:** (1, 2, 3). **117 Jens Jakobsen:** (t, b). **119 Jens Jakobsen:** (t, b). **120 Alamy Stock Photo:** Bailey-Cooper Photography (br); Johner Images (bc). **GAP Photos:** GAP Photos - Designer: Tom Massey (bl). **121 Alamy Stock Photo:** Bailey-Cooper Photography (3/b); Harry Wedzinga (1/bl); VPales (2/b). **GAP Photos:** Paul Debois (4/b). **126 Shutterstock.com:** Hurst Photo. **129 Shutterstock.com:** Hurst Photo. **135 Sin Roe:** Sin Roe. **136 Alamy Stock Photo:** Andrew Brooks (2); Wild Birds, Alius Imago (1); Westend61 GmbH (3). **138 Alamy Stock Photo:** MitarArt. **139 Alamy Stock Photo:** Andrew Brooks. **140 Shutterstock.com:** Hurst Photo. **141 Shutterstock.com:** Hurst Photo. **142 Dorling Kindersley:** Mark Winwood / Downderry Nursery (bl). **158 The Ron Finley Project:** Ron Finley (2); Kat Hanegraaf (1). **159 The Ron Finley Project:** Michael Armenta (b); Dallas Logan (t). **160 The Ron Finley Project:** Michael Armenta. **163 Shutterstock.com:** Hurst Photo.

**Cover images:** *Front:* **Alamy Stock Photo:** Lorraine Mitchell bl/1; **Getty Images / iStock:** George Clerk br

All other images © Sebatian Barros

### DK LONDON

**Editorial Manager** Ruth O'Rourke
**Project Editor** Lucy Philpott
**Senior US Editor** Megan Douglass
**Senior Designer** Tania Gomes
**Editorial Assistant** Charlotte Beauchamp
**Senior Production Editor** Tony Phipps
**Senior Production Controller** Stephanie McConnell
**Jacket and Sales Material Coordinator** Emily Cannings
**Art Director** Maxine Pedliham
**Publishing Director** Katie Cowan

**Editorial** Joanna Chisholm
**Design** Stuart Tolley
**Photography** Sebastian Barros
**Collage illustration** Barbara Gibson and Marta Kochanek
**Consultant Gardening Publisher** Chris Young

First American Edition, 2024
Published in the United States by DK Publishing
1754 Broadway, 20th Floor, New York, NY 10019

Text copyright © Tayshan Hayden-Smith 2024
Photography copyright © Sebastian Barros, 2024
Copyright © 2024 Dorling Kindersley Limited
DK, A division of Penguin Random House LLC
24 25 26 27 28 10 9 8 7 6 5 4 3 2 1
001–335290–Apr/2024

A catalog record for this book
is available from the Library of Congress.
ISBN: 978-0-7440-9233-2

Printed and bound in China

**www.dk.com**